GETTYSBURG

THE PIVOTAL BATTLE OF THE CIVIL WAR

MAJ.-GEN. GEORGE G. MEADE

Com. Army of the Potomac, June, 1863 — June, 1865

GETTYSBURG

THE PIVOTAL BATTLE OF THE CIVIL WAR

BY

CAPTAIN R. K. BEECHAM

OF THE FIRST BRIGADE, FIRST DIVISION, FIRST CORPS,
ARMY OF THE POTOMAC

WITH ILLUSTRATIONS

1994

A Platinum Press Book

This special reprint edition originally published
in 1911 is now republished by:

Longmeadow Press
201 High Ridge Road
Stamford, CT 06904

in association with

Platinum Press Inc.
311 Crossways Park Drive
Woodbury, NY 11797

Longmeadow Press and the colophon are registered trademarks.

ISBN 0-681-00758-3

0987654321

Printed in the USA

Library of Congress Cataloging-in-Publication Data

Beechman, R. K.
    Gettysburg : the pivotal battle of the Civil War / by R. K.
Beechman
        p. cm.
    Originally published : Chicago : A. C. McClurg, 1911.
    "A Platinum Press book."
    Includes index.
    ISBN 0-681-00758-3
    1. Gettysburg (Pa.), Battle of, 1863 — Personal narratives.
2. United States. Army. Iron Brigade (1861-1865)   3. Beechman,
R.K. I. Title.
E475.53.B4 1994
973.7'349 — dc20   94-14472
                                                                  CIP

CONTENTS

CONTENTS—Continued

APPENDIX

GETTYSBURG

THE PIVOTAL BATTLE OF THE CIVIL WAR

CHAPTER I

THE VETERAN'S MECCA

IN the month of May and in the last year of the nineteenth century, an old man, dusty and travel-stained, changed cars at Hagerstown, Maryland, and rode northeastward over a spur of the Blue Ridge Range, called the South Mountain.

The old man wore a small bronze button in the lapel of his coat, and from that, with other personal characteristics, it was plain that he was an ex-Union soldier of the great American Civil War. He was wonderfully interested in observing the face of the country, and his interest increased as the train crossed the State line into Pennsylvania. He seemed to be watching for some familiar landmark.

Shortly after crossing the State line the train turned eastward, and a few minutes later crossed a creek or run, beyond which, to the north side of the track, stood a bronze equestrian statue, with a long line of granite monuments extending to the northeast, while to the southward of the track the same line of monuments continued, apparently without limit.

As the train passed through the line of monuments the old soldier watched them from the car windows with an eager eye, and carefully noted the lay of the land on either side, as if the hills and valleys were the familiar haunts of his boyhood.

Then the train ran through a deep cut across a high ridge, coming out on the eastern side into a beautiful valley, across which, from west to east, extended a continuation of the line of monuments intersected by the railroad on the west side of the ridge; and a moment later, as the train drew up to the station in the outskirts of the fair city that nestled peacefully among the green hills of Pennsylvania, the brakeman called aloud — "Gettysburg!"

At this point our traveller left the train. He was a Gettysburg veteran, returning after many years to revisit the city and sojourn for a season among the fields where the life of the United States of America was saved, and where as a young man of twenty-five, he had fought in defence of the Old Flag and for the perpetuation of the Union.

In 1863, until after the Battle of Gettysburg was fought and won, the United States of America was looked upon by the nations of Europe as in the last throes of national dissolution, and "Bull-Run Russell's" statement, thundered forth through the *London Times*, "The foundation stones of the young American Republic are falling to pieces," was taken by the world at large as literally true.

There were then within and without the American Union thirty-five States, — including West Virginia, which was admitted into the Union in 1863, — but of these thirty-five States, eleven had seceded from the Union and were then in open rebellion, waging a war of awful bitterness for what they termed their "freedom from oppression"; and by all that was good and great they had vowed that neither force nor favour could compel or induce them to return to, or become again a part of, the hateful old Union. There were also three or four other States very anxious to follow the example of their wayward sisters, which were kept within the Union only by the force of arms. Thus it becomes evident that the men who fought beneath the Stars and Stripes at Gettysburg contended for and defended the very existence of the United States of America.

In making this pilgrimage to his Mecca the veteran had travelled far, but though dust-begrimed, he felt no weariness. He had started from the shore of Puget Sound, that wonderful inland sea of the young Northwest, scarcely known or heard of in the days of the Civil War; and not on foot did he travel, as in his first weary march, but in a flying chariot, along the steel rails that span the continent, he crossed the States of Washington, Idaho, Montana, North Dakota, Minnesota, Wisconsin, Illinois,

Indiana, Ohio, West Virginia, Maryland, and into Pennsylvania — twelve of the forty-five States that in the last year of the nineteenth century constituted our great and matchless American Union. Then, too, was our nation at peace throughout her borders; and not a single State of the whole forty-five wanted to secede from the Union, but all were contented and prosperous.

In making that flying trip, in a little less than five days, the old man crossed the great mountain ranges of the continent; travelled plains where millions of cattle pasture and fatten; threaded forests dark and deep and apparently without limit; rode among fields that produce the bread of the nation; and visited cities that swell and rejoice with the arts of peace and the onward rush of civilization.

In his pathway were the rivers of America — the Snohomish, the Skikomish, the Wenatchie, the Columbia, the Spokane, the Missouri, the Red, the Mississippi, the Wisconsin, the Ohio, the Potomac; and rivers, cities, fields, forests, plains, and mountains were all a part, and only a part, of "Our Country." For two thousand miles he coursed along

[13]

the northern rim and then dashed southeastward for another thousand miles toward the capital of this great country that we proudly call, and hope it shall ever be, " The Land of the Free," which certainly still contains more of the blessings of liberty and the enjoyments of life than can be found in any other land upon which the light of the sun descends.

Is it strange that the veteran felt no weariness of body or soul when he arrived at last at his Mecca, in the happy days of peace ?

PRESIDENT ABRAHAM LINCOLN

GENERAL ULYSSES S. GRANT

CHAPTER II

I N the days of the old veteran's first pilgrimage to Gettysburg there was war in the land, bloody and terrible war; and the end thereof seemed farther away, the result more uncertain, than in the beginning. The United States apparently had made slow progress, or rather no progress at all, toward suppressing the rebellion. Though the North was superior in population and possessed greater wealth and more abundance of war material, there were other causes and circumstances that for a long time tended to equalize the war-strength of the two sections.

During the years of the agitation of Secession the Southland had made greater preparation for war than had the United States Government, and from the beginning of the war the Confederate armies possessed the advantages of a semi-military training that the armies of the United States lacked.

It is true that slavery never gave substantial wealth to any people, ancient or modern; but it has always built up an aristocratic class, with sufficient wealth and leisure to prepare them for leadership; and splendid military leaders they made. In our Southland, before the war, nearly all the sons of planters were educated in military tactics, horsemanship, target practice, and feats of arms. They had a pride of birth and a certain arrogance which qualified them to command men in war, and they were a superb body of officers in the Confederate armies, from Robert E. Lee down to their second lieutenants.

Then the men who stood behind the guns in their battle-lines had received certain peculiar qualifications for soldiers through that same teacher. The majority of the men in the Confederate ranks were of the "poor white" class who owned not a single slave,—many of them not even a mule,—but every man of them owned a rifle, by which, to a great extent, he made his living. Slavery had made it dishonourable for a white man to work at honest labour, and thereby had driven thousands to subsist chiefly by their skill as hunters. Their marksmanship was almost perfect, and when the call to arms came, they had the skill to shoot and needed no training in the use of firearms. They were brave as hunters proverbially are; obedient to their superiors as soldiers; inured to all manner of hardship and exposure; and they could stand up in battle-line and shoot with the best trained soldiers in the world. How could it be otherwise than that such a soldiery weighed mightily in the war-scale of the Southland ?

On the other hand, the Northern soldiery went into the war reluctantly, to save the integrity of the Union. They were men of peace; there were few hunters among them, even from the West, and in many whole regiments there was scarcely a man who had ever before handled a gun; as an army they were comparatively deficient in marksmanship, and required much training and practice ere they became efficient soldiers. But few of the officers of the Union armies were gentlemen of leisure before the war, and generally they lacked every element of military training.

GETTYSBURG

The North had two-thirds of the white population; but the tactics of the Confederacy compelled the Northern armies to climb every hill and mountain range, cross every stream and river, attack every natural stronghold that afforded protection, and meet them everywhere in their chosen positions of defence.

There were also two conditions that found place in the Army of the Potomac that must be noticed here, as they had much to do with the prolongation of the war. First, in the Winter of 1861-62, General George B. McClellan spent months in organizing and drilling an army of more than a hundred thousand men. McClellan was an organizer, whatever may be said of his generalship; but he was also a lover of style, and delighted greatly in grand reviews and showy parades, which were of little or no use in the field where battles are to be lost or won. Nor was McClellan the only general that doted on style, his subordinate generals being about equal to him in their inordinate love for display. Sunday morning inspection was attended to with surpassing particularity; but if a single general or colonel in that vast army ever made the discovery that a soldier could have a clean and presentable gun on inspection without having that gun polished to a finish brightness, no soldier in the Army of the Potomac ever heard of it. The consequence was that during that winter the Army of the Potomac wore to a frazzle more than a hundred thousand guns by the too free use of sandpaper, and the Northern war-scale was thereby lightened thirty or forty per cent for the Spring campaign of 1862; and in such circumstances how could McClellan have been expected to win battles?

Later, after the army took the field, the soldiers learned for themselves and put in practice, in caring for their arms, the common-sense ideas that every hunter knows; and after the Army of the Potomac had been supplied with new arms all around, it stood some show in the field of war.

The other circumstance, which was even more serious in reducing the weight of the Union war-scale, and in giving additional weight to that of the enemy, remained with us to the end of the war. The old veteran did not discover this latter evil and fraud that was practised on the Army of the Potomac and on the Nation, until after the beginning of the campaign of 1862, and he has no means of knowing the whole extent of the evil. The discovery was made by the soldiers themselves, and was verified hundreds of times before the war ended, that the powder used in our infantry ammunition was of the poorest quality — so dirty and so nearly void of strength in many instances as to be next to valueless; while the Confederate powder, often examined and tested, was invariably found to have two-fold the explosive power of ours.

CHAPTER III

THERE was war in the land, and that war
had been in progress for a period of more
than two years, during which time many battles
had been fought and much blood sacrificed without
any apparent gain, on the part of the Union cause.
Few indeed were the battles won, especially in the
East, where the Army of the Potomac was pitted
against the Army of Northern Virginia, and every
Union campaign, except one, had been a failure.

In every campaign, except one, the Army of the
Potomac had assumed the offensive; but, by the
superior genius of its great commander, the Army
of Northern Virginia had succeeded in putting it
first on the defensive, after which soon followed
defeat. That exception was when Lee, assuming
the offensive, crossed the Potomac River into Maryland, where he in turn was put on the defensive and

defeated at Antietam by the Army of the Potomac under the command of General McClellan, and compelled to retreat to his strongholds in Virginia.

This victory at Antietam gave President Lincoln the opportunity which he had long desired, of issuing his Emancipation Proclamation, hoping thereby to strengthen the Union cause and correspondingly weaken the cause of the Confederacy by inducing certain of the slave States to accept compensation for their slaves and return to the Union. Therefore, he left the proclamation open until January 1, 1863. However, Lincoln's action seemed at first to weaken the Union cause. Lee retreated across the Potomac, and from the Potomac to his old defensive line south of the Rappahannock, where, on the thirteenth of December was fought the useless and murderous battle of Fredericksburg. How or why the authorities at Washington concluded to fight a battle, or allowed a battle to be fought, as late in the season as December, is beyond all comprehension; also, why Lincoln, as Commander-in-Chief, should have been blind to the fact that our army was worn out, and needed rest and thorough reorganization; and that with the Rappahannock in its front and the Potomac as a convenient base, there was the ideal place, not to fight a battle in December, but to prepare the army for battle in the season for battles. Why any general with a grain of military knowledge in his head should not have seen that nothing could be gained even by a victory in mid-winter with such roads and such a climate to contend against as Virginia furnished, passes all understanding. But the battle was ordered and fought, and the Army of the Potomac was defeated with terrible slaughter.

Then followed for the Army of the Potomac the midnight of war, the darkest period of its existence. Many officers talked open treason, while in the ranks men reviled the Government, and nearly all seemed to agree that the war for the Union had degenerated into a "war for the nigger." The demoralization increased after the Emancipation Proclamation was issued, on January 1, 1863, and it reached its most appalling stage about January twentieth, when Burnside made another attempt at a winter campaign, which was brought to an end by a providential rain that deluged the land and made the roads impassable. Oh, that blessed rain ! The campaign was short, but long remembered as "Burnside stuck in the mud."

The Emancipation Proclamation then came in for its full share of abuse and ridicule; "Old Abe's Folly" was jeered by every lawyer in the army, and among our officers we had many lawyers. They argued that the proclamation could serve no good purpose and would never emancipate a single slave. But there were some anti-slavery men in the army, who believed from the beginning that slavery was the cause of the war, and must end with the war; and they said: "It is up to the army. If rebellion wins, emancipation is a dead letter; but if we put down the rebellion, as we started out to do, and intend to do, the Emancipation Proclamation will free every slave in America."

On the twenty-seventh of January, General Joseph Hooker was assigned to the command of the Army of the Potomac. Hooker was a fighting general, but he recognized the fact that an army — as shown by the rolls — with 2,922 officers and

GETTYSBURG

81,964 soldiers absent in hospitals or on leave or from desertion, needed rest and reorganization before any more serious fighting began; and for the next three months he applied himself to that task, which, to his credit, he accomplished so thoroughly that thereafter the Army of the Potomac never wavered in its discipline.

Early in May the Spring campaign opened; but that splendid army of 123,000 men that Hooker led into battle south of the Rappahannock was, by the superior generalship of Lee, put upon the defensive, defeated, and compelled to retreat to its former position north of the river.

Chancellorsville was Lee's greatest military achievement; but the defeat of the Army of the Potomac at that time, though very discouraging to the Administration, did not seem to affect in the least degree the morale of the army. Thereafter the soldiers sang as of old their songs of love, and their songs of war, but it was not until after Gettysburg that they began to sing—

> " John Brown's body lies mouldering in the grave,
> But his soul is marching on! "

GETTYSBURG

From that date, however, until the end of the war, in camp, on the march, before and after battle, the hills of Virginia rang with the refrain —

" Glory, glory, halleluiah! Glory, glory, halleluiah!
Glory, glory, halleluiah! His soul is marching on! "

CHAPTER IV

COMPARATIVE STRENGTH OF THE ARMIES

AFTER winning two great victories, like Fredericksburg and Chancellorsville, it is not to be wondered at that Lee should consider the Army of Northern Virginia, under his command and leadership, as invincible. Therefore, immediately after the latter battle, Lee, with the consent and enthusiastic coöperation of Jefferson Davis and the whole Confederate Government, began to plan and prepare for a second invasion of the North. For the purpose of that invasion Lee reorganized his army, intending if possible to make his second invasion more successful than the first; and we may be certain that he made every effort in his power to enable him to lead that army to victory. He did not invade the North with the intention of being defeated in his first battle across the line and turned back to his old, familiar stamping ground, if he could help it.

On May thirtieth, Lee issued an order reorganizing his army, which at that time consisted of two corps, commanded respectively by James Longstreet and A. P. Hill. According to his field report of that date — the last field return of record from Lee's army previous to the Battle of Gettysburg — the total strength of those two corps and his cavalry was as follows:

Longstreet's Corps	**30,732**
Hill's Corps	**32,588**
Stuart's Cavalry Corps . . .	**10,292**

Total Infantry, Artillery, and Cavalry, **73,612**

We have no certain and accurate account of the strength of Lee's army after it was reorganized into three corps, but it does not seem reasonable to presume that he reorganized his army into three corps just for ostentation. Lee was not built that way. He reorganized his army into three corps in order to add to its efficiency; and he then and there and thereafter added every regiment and every man that the Confederate Government would give him, and it gladly gave him every man obtainable. Lee was about to undertake a great enterprise — nothing short of an invasion of the North, which he hoped, and the Confederate Government confidently expected, would result in a great and sweeping victory, leading directly to an acknowledgment of the Confederacy by the nations of Europe. Is it at all reasonable to suppose that he would undertake such a stupendous work without first obtaining what he considered reasonable and adequate reinforcements ? It is fair to presume that in adding to his army a third corps, he thereby materially increased its numerical strength.

Whatever the full strength of Lee's army of invasion may have been, Lee himself and the Confederate Government also were extremely careful that the world should not know with any degree of certainty what it was, and to this day it remains a sealed book. Still we do know of a certainty that the corps, divisions, brigades, and regiments of Lee's army, as reorganized for the great campaign that terminated in the Battle of Gettysburg, were each and all stronger than the corresponding organizations in the Army of the Potomac. While

Lee's army was composed of three corps, the Union army was composed of seven; while Lee's army comprised thirty-nine brigades of infantry, the Army of the Potomac comprised fifty-one brigades.

The unit of both armies was the regiment, and in that respect the Confederate army had a decided advantage over the Union army. The regimental formation was the same, but the Confederacy adopted a different method of adding recruits.

The Confederacy, while it lasted, was a military organization, pure and complete; and at the very start their military leaders determined that everything else should bow to the efficiency of their army. Therefore, after the second year of the war they added very few new regiments. Instead, they almost robbed the cradle and the grave for recruits to fill up their armies, but instead of making up full regiments entirely of raw and unseasoned men, they divided them up among the old regiments long in the field, wherein every private soldier was as good or better than an officer of a new regiment. Usually, an old regiment of three hundred experienced men is worth more in battle than a new regiment of nine hundred. Take a regiment reduced by hard service to two hundred men, or twenty to the company; increase it to three hundred by adding ten recruits to each company; within a week or ten days the whole three hundred are veterans, and the recruits are about as good as the best of them. In that way five hundred recruits are better for an army than two full regiments of a thousand men each, fresh from civil life with no military experience.

The Confederate leaders had sense enough to discover that fact early in the war, and they proceeded at once to put their knowledge into practice anywhere and everywhere along military lines, paying no regard whatever to the whims of those who knew nothing about war, but who thought perhaps some other way might possibly be an improvement.

With the Union army it was different. It is doubtful if any of our military authorities ever learned the superiority of the system of sending recruits to old regiments in the field, over adding entirely new regiments; and if they did they could not, or at least did not, put it into practice to any extent. Up to the last year and last month of the

war, the State authorities recruited full regiments
of green troops and sent them to the front in great
unwieldy bodies to fill up the armies, while the old
and experienced regiments dwindled into nothing-
ness. That plan furnished official positions for
political pets, most of whom were worthless as soldiers in any position, but it did not do the best that
could be done for the army. If one of these full
regiments was added to a brigade, it outnumbered
the old four regiments combined; but in the first
battle any one of the first regiments with a hundred
men or less, was usually worth the most. The new
regiment would soon become a power in the brigade,
but at a terrible sacrifice of life. When reduced to
about five hundred men, that regiment was at its
best, and became the backbone of the brigade. By
their system of filling up their old regiments, the
Confederates kept them at all times at very nearly
their fighting weight, which, as we have stated, was
about five hundred men to the regiment; and as each
brigade in both armies contained four or five regiments, it is easy to understand how even a slight
difference in the numerical strength of the units

created a difference in all the organizations above the unit.

These facts present the opportunity of making a comparative estimate of the strength of Lee's army in the Gettysburg campaign that cannot be far from correct. In the Union army we had fifty-one brigades, and a total strength of infantry of 77,208, or an average of 1,514 men to the brigade. In Lee's army there were thirty-nine brigades of infantry, which reasonably averaged eighteen hundred or two thousand men to the brigade; and if the latter, which was less than several of them numbered, Lee's total infantry strength was about 78,-000. But if we estimate the average of Lee's brigades at the former figure of eighteen hundred, it would still give him a total of 70,200 infantry, besides his artillery and cavalry.

The fact is, however, that there are no means of ascertaining the exact strength of Lee's army. Longstreet gives his estimate at 75,568, which is probably as accurate as any to be obtained from a Confederate source; but as Longstreet estimates the Army of the Potomac at more than one hundred thousand, we must take his figures with a grain of allowance.

With regard to the strength of the Army of the Potomac, there can be no question. General Meade, in his testimony before the Congressional Committee on the Conduct of the War, stated the strength of his army at "a little under 100,000 — probably 95,000 men." That estimate was very nearly correct, as the returns of June 30, 1863, of the Army of the Potomac, "present for duty equipped," shows as follows:

First Corps	10,022
Second Corps	12,904
Third Corps	11,924
Fifth Corps	12,509
Sixth Corps	15,555
Eleventh Corps	9,841
Twelfth Corps	8,589
Reserve Artillery	2,546
Cavalry Corps	10,809
Total, ...	94,699

It is an easy matter to verify these figures. They are of record in the War Department of the United

States. We know to an absolute certainty the strength of the Army of the Potomac, and from all the knowledge we are able to glean on the subject we conclude that the contending armies, commanded respectively by Generals Meade and Lee, were numerically about equal. At all events Lee was satisfied that his army was in many respects superior to the Union army opposed to him, and his generals looked upon the Army of Northern Virginia as then marshalled, equipped, and led, as invincible. It was, as General Gordon described it, "in the zenith of assurance, with compact ranks, boundless confidence, and exultant hopes, as proud and puissant an army as was ever marshalled."

CHAPTER V

MANY people do not readily understand why it was that in the concentration of the opposing armies for battle, the Army of Northern Virginia, commanded by Lee, which was the army of invasion, advanced from the *north* toward Gettysburg; while the Army of the Potomac, commanded by Meade, which was the defensive or repelling army, moved up from the *south* to meet the invading army and give, or rather receive, battle. The positions in which we find the two armies at this time can be explained only by a brief outline of their previous movements. Lee's main army crossed the Potomac River into Maryland at Williamsport, on the twenty-fourth and twenty-fifth days of June, 1863, with the exception of the main body of his cavalry, under the command of Stuart. Lee had instructed Stuart to cover his movements, to deceive Hooker as long as possible with regard to Lee's whereabouts, and to prevent the Army of the Potomac from crossing the river in pursuit, while he secured favourable offensive positions for his army.

Previous to this, on the fifteenth of June, General Ewell, with the Second Corps of Lee's army and two brigades of cavalry, crossed the Potomac at the same point; Ewell sent his cavalry in advance, up the Cumberland Valley as far as Chambersburg, while he moved leisurely with his infantry, gathering supplies of flour and beef-cattle for the army, also replenishing his supply of mules and draft horses from the farmers of that region. He also raised all the ready money he could by assessing the towns and cities along his route. Ewell had ten days in which to operate against a peaceful country, without so much as a regiment of soldiers to oppose his free hand, before Lee made his crossing, and by that time was well up the Cumberland Valley with his whole corps. On crossing the Potomac with his main army Lee immediately concentrated at Hagerstown, six miles north of the river and seventy-four miles southwest of Harrisburg, the capital of Pennsylvania, which city Lee proposed to make his first objective point. There was no army in his front except his own Second Corps, nothing to interfere with his onward march; and Ewell had already gathered and stored at convenient points the supplies necessary for his army. No general ever had a more complete and delightful walk-away; and taking advantage of this most favourable situation, he lost not a moment but dashed through the Cumberland Valley, intending to reach and cross the Susquehanna River and capture Harrisburg. He also directed Ewell to cross the South Mountain into the Susquehanna Valley and occupy all the important points and all the roads leading southward from Harrisburg. In this movement Early, with Ewell's first division, crossed the mountains by the Chambersburg Pike, passing through Gettysburg on the afternoon of the twenty-sixth of June, which town he assessed to the tune of ten thousand dollars; which little amount he failed to collect, either on account of the poverty of the business men of Gettysburg, or their "pull" with the Confederate authorities. We were told by old residents of Gettysburg that before the war the town had enjoyed great prosperity through certain Southern business houses, and that at the time of the battle it was Pennsylvania's hotbed of secession. We cannot vouch for the truth of this report, but if ture, it would readily account for some other incidents besides the fact that Early failed to get his ten-thousand-dollar assessment. From Gettysburg Early marched northeast on the York Pike to the town of York, where he was more fortunate in his financial schemes; he succeeded in raising some money, assessing that city at one hundred thousand dollars, part of which he collected.

General Gordon says *: " Early wanted to borrow, or secure in some other way, for the use of his troops, a certain amount of greenbacks, and he succeeded in making the arrangement. I learned afterwards that the only promise to pay, like that of the Confederate notes, was at some date subsequent to the establishment of Southern independence." Probably nothing in Gordon's memoirs of Gettysburg is more pointedly true in every particu-

---

* From " Reminiscences," by Gen. John B. Gordon, copyrighted by Messrs. Charles Scribner's Sons.

lar than this explanation of Early's financial deal at York.

To throw some further light on the patriotic spirit that to some extent pervaded that portion of Pennsylvania, against which the Union army had to contend even in the North, we will again quote the words of General Gordon, in his York experience:

" As we moved along the street, a little girl, probably twelve years of age, ran up to my horse and handed me a large bouquet of flowers, in the centre of which was a note in delicate handwriting, purporting to give the numbers and describe the position of the Union forces at Wrightsville, toward which I was advancing. I carefully read and reread this strange note. It bore no signature and contained no assurance of sympathy for the Southern cause, but it was so terse and explicit in its terms as to compel my confidence. The second day we were in front of Wrightsville, and from the high ridge on which this note suggested that I halt and examine the position of the Union troops, I eagerly scanned the prospect with my field-glasses, in order to verify the truth of the mysterious communication, or detect its misrepresentation. There, in full view before us, was the town, just as described, nestling on the banks of the Susquehanna. There was the blue line of soldiers guarding the approach, drawn up as indicated, along the intervening ridge and across the pike. There was the long bridge spanning the Susquehanna and connecting the town with Columbia on the other bank. Most important of all, there was the gorge or ravine running off to the right and extending around the left flank of the Federal line and to the river below the bridge. Not an inaccurate detail in that note could be discovered. I did not hesitate, therefore, to adopt its suggestion of moving down the gorge in order to throw my command on the flank, or possibly in the rear of the Union troops, and force them to a rapid retreat or surrender. The result of this movement vindicated the strategic wisdom of my unknown, and — judging by the handwriting — female correspondent, whose note was none the less martial because embedded in roses, and whose evident genius for war, had occasion offered, might have made her a captain equal to Catherine. . . .

"It will be remembered that the note concealed in the flowers handed me at York had indicated a ravine down which I could move, reaching the river not far from the bridge. As my orders were not restricted, except to direct me to cross the Susquehanna if possible, my immediate object was to move rapidly down that ravine to the river, then along its right bank to the bridge, seize it, and cross to the Columbia side. Once across, I intended to mount my men, if practicable, so as to pass rapidly through Lancaster in the direction of Philadelphia, and thus compel General Meade to send a portion of his army to defend that city. This programme was defeated, first, by the burning of the bridge; and, second, by the imminent prospect of battle near Gettysburg. The Union troops stationed at Wrightsville had, in their retreat across it, fired the bridge which I had hoped to secure."

Besides Gordon's story of the note in the bouquet, which is certainly more interesting than anything the author could say in its place, the side-light thrown on the history of that campaign and on the position of the Confederate army at that time by the foregoing quotation is well worth utilizing here.

[41]

The reader will notice that Gordon, commanding a brigade of Lee's Second Corps, had reached the Susquehanna River at Wrightsville, below Harrisburg, when Lee's concentration order reached him. Returning now to Lee's main army as it moved along the Cumberland Valley from Chambersburg northeast toward the Susquehanna River, we note that everything was working beautifully for Lee. The capital of Pennsylvania was almost within his grasp. Just a few more days, and the first great stroke of his campaign of invasion would be accomplished. It was at that time that Longstreet's scout, Harrison, brought the news to Lee's headquarters that Hooker had outmanœuvred Stuart, and with his whole army had crossed the Potomac at Point of Rocks and Edwards's Ferry, on the twenty-fifth and twenty-sixth of June, and was then in hot pursuit. These tidings from out the South troubled Lee, for he saw and clearly comprehended the fact that the Army of the Potomac must be taken into immediate consideration. Furthermore Lee learned that on the twenty-sixth of June Hooker had discovered the unprotected condition of his line of communications, and would have drawn the garrison from Harper's Ferry to act with the Twelfth Corps to strike Lee's trains exposed from the Potomac to Chambersburg. Halleck would not give his consent to the withdrawal of the Harper's Ferry garrison, which piece of foolishness saved Lee's trains. The disagreement of Halleck and Hooker on the matter of the Harper's Ferry garrison caused the resignation of Hooker and the appointment of Meade to the command of the Army of the Potomac. Hooker was clearly right in his contention, and Halleck was wrong — as he usually was — but it served as an excuse to get rid of Hooker. Meade was allowed to withdraw the garrison, but before he had time to move on Lee's trains and communications, Lee had seen the necessity of turning in his tracks. He therefore abandoned his attack on Harrisburg; leaving the Cumberland Valley, he marched eastward across the South Mountain into the valley of the Susquehanna, and on the night of the thirtieth of June, his army was located about as follows: Early's division on the York Pike, fifteen miles northeast of Gettysburg; Johnson's division eighteen miles northeast, on the Harrisburg Road; Rodes' division ten miles north, on the Carlisle Road; Pender's division eight miles northwest, on the Mummasburg Road; Heth's division five miles northwest on the Chambersburg Pike; and from that point to Chambersburg in a continuous line west for twenty or twenty-five miles lay the balance of Lee's army, thus covering the whole country and every highway for the distance of about forty miles east and west, and every one of those highways converging at Gettysburg.

On the other hand the Union army, which had crossed the Potomac one day later than Lee's army, and fully fifty miles south and east, with a mountain range between, had marched northward, spreading out like a fan to the eastward in order to present a barrier between Lee's army and our national capital.

On June twenty-eighth, General Meade was assigned to the command of the army. He continued our march to the northward; and, on the night of June thirtieth Buford's cavalry division occupied a position northwest of Gettysburg, with headquarters at the Lutheran Seminary on Semi-

nary Ridge, his troops picketing the Chambersburg
Pike and the Mummasburg Road, and guarding
the crossings of Willoughby Run, within an hour's
march of Heth's outposts of Lee's foremost division.
Our First Corps, commanded by General Doubleday, was at Marsh Creek, six miles from Buford's
position. Howard, with the Eleventh Corps, was
at Emmetsburg, thirteen miles away. Sickles'
Third Corps was somewhere between Emmetsburg
and Taneytown, probably about the same distance
away as the Eleventh. These three corps, with
Buford's cavalry division, made up the right wing
of the Army of the Potomac commanded by General Reynolds. Beyond Sickles' corps the balance
of the Union army lay stretched away to the southeast along the Taneytown Road and Baltimore
Pike for a distance of thirty or forty miles.

General Meade had established his headquarters
at or near Taneytown, and was supervising the survey, through his chief engineer, of a position on
Pipe Creek two miles south of Taneytown, that
seemed to him a choice position for a defensive battle, and there he hoped to await Lee's advance and

attack. His army was scattered from Dan to Beer-sheba, so to speak, his idea being to concentrate at this point when he found Lee, and if possible to induce Lee to follow his retreating forces to his chosen position. Such were the comparative positions and dispositions of the opposing armies and their commanding generals on the night before the great battle — the Southern army to the northward and the Northern army to the southward — from which positions they advanced toward each other, meeting in their appalling death-grapple at Gettysburg.

CHAPTER VI

I T is said that before the great battle of Marathon the Greeks and the Persians stood in battle array for days before the battle opened, each army manœuvring for some position of advantage; Miltiades not caring to leave his strong position on the heights to attack the Persians who darkened the plain below, and Darius not relishing the risk of attacking the Greeks in their strong and well-chosen position. The Persians were ready for battle from the start, as Darius had a mighty army and every regiment in place. He was not waiting for reinforcements, but for sand. The Greeks were few, and Miltiades wanted every Greek he could get; but when he was reinforced by a thousand heavy-armed Platæans, he took the chances and ordered the Greeks to wade in, which they did, with good results for the Greeks.

GETTYSBURG

At Waterloo the English held the heights, the French occupying the low ground, but both armies camped on the field the night before the battle; for we are told that at one o'clock A.M. on the eighteenth of June, 1815, Napoleon, while exploring on horseback the hills near Rassomme, in the tempest and in the rain, was gratified "to see the long line of English camp fires illuminating all the horizon from Frischemont to Braine l'Allend." Napoleon was gratified to know the English were there, and he considered them as his meat; but when the morning dawned he was in no hurry to attack. It had rained during the night and the grass that grew luxuriantly on the Belgian hillsides was wet and difficult for his soldiers to wade through,— Napoleon always had a tender spot in his heart for his soldiers,— so it was half-past eleven o'clock before the first gun was fired at Waterloo. Both armies were ready for battle, and had been for hours, but appeared not anxious to engage. Sometimes opposing armies do not form in battle array and wait for each other, until everything is in readiness on both sides, and then at an apparently agreed signal they join issue all along the line.

At Gettysburg the conditions were different. Here were two armies, each nearly 100,000 strong, drawing toward each other and anxious to engage in deadly strife — so anxious that neither was ready for battle when it began; they were destined to join battle on this field, and yet, with the exception of Buford's little band of cavalry watching the crossings of Willoughby Run, the heights and the valleys were vacant. Where were the armies ? When the Battle of Gettysburg opened on the morning of the first of July between the heads of the leading columns, the main portions of the armies were from twenty to fifty miles apart.

The advantages were greatly in Lee's favour. He had his army comparatively well in hand. He had seven highways at his service, all converging at his rendezvous, to facilitate the movement of his troops. He had issued his orders of concentration to his corps and divisions, and each was marching by the shortest route to the point designated; and when the head of his foremost division under Heth encountered Buford's cavalry on the banks of Willoughby Run, the rear of his outmost column was not more than twenty-five miles away.

For Meade the situation was most unfavourable. While Buford occupied the vantage ground of camping on the outskirts of the field, and was awaiting the advance of Lee upon his lines, he could not hope for support from Meade's main army in that position. Meade had not ordered the advance and concentration of his army at that or any other point; in fact he was in ignorance of the whereabouts and the movements of his adversary, and with headquarters at Taneytown, fifteen miles away, was waiting for Lee to come and find him.

General Reynolds, who commanded the right wing of the Army of the Potomac, had sent Buford forward to his advanced position and had ordered the First Corps at Marsh Creek, and the Eleventh Corps at Emmetsburg, to move in the same direction at an early hour on the morning of July first.

When Buford was attacked, Reynolds hurried forward the First and Eleventh Corps to his support, and also sent a despatch to General Meade at

Taneytown, telling him that Lee's forces were in front of him; that he would hold the key to the situation till the last moment, and until the main army should arrive, and that the heights of Gettysburg was the place to fight the battle.

About twenty minutes past eight o'clock A.M., July first, Heth's division encountered Buford's pickets and opened the battle. An hour later the First Corps, under Doubleday, began to arrive, reinforcing Buford. Another hour and Pender's division of Lee's army reinforces Heth. About noon, or a little later, Rodes' division arrives from the north and is extending Heth's lines eastward, when Howard's Eleventh Corps of the Union army comes up from the south reinforcing Doubleday and Buford, and engaging Rodes, to the north of the city. All this time the battle is in progress. An hour or two later Early's division from the northeast reinforces Rodes, turning the tide of battle against the Union army.

At four o'clock P.M. Howard and Doubleday withdraw their shattered columns to Cemetery Hill, where at about five o'clock they are reinforced by

Slocum's Twelfth Corps, and about the same time General Hancock arrives on Cemetery Hill; Meade having received Reynolds' despatch and sending Hancock forward to inspect the field and report the situation.

Night declares a truce to the battle, but not to the marching. Before morning dawns, Lee's army is all in line except Pickett's division and Stuart's cavalry, while Lee himself has established his headquarters at or near the Lutheran Seminary. Hancock has reported to Meade his approval of the position then being held for the continuation of the battle. Meade has accepted Hancock's report as final; has ordered his whole army to concentrate at Gettysburg, and has established his headquarters just in rear or south of Cemetery Hill, arriving in person about midnight. The Second Corps, commanded by Hancock, has reached the field and prolonged Meade's line to the left. Sickles' Third Corps is also on the ground ready to take position in the line. Still the Fifth and Sixth Corps, numbering 28,000 men, or more than a third of Meade's army, are absent. With the coming of day, the manœuvring for position begins. Neither army seems as anxious for battle as it was the day before. They adopt the tactics of the Greeks and Persians at Marathon for many hours. In the afternoon, however, the battle opens again with great fury, and continues until after dark. Just before sunset Meade is reinforced by the fifth, and a little later by the third division of the Sixth Corps.

Again night puts an end to the carnage. During the night of July second, Pickett's division and Stuart's cavalry reinforce Lee's army; he then has at his command the whole Army of Northern Virginia, while the first and second divisions of the Sixth Corps arrive, making the Army of the Potomac complete.

When dawns the morning of July third, the two armies face each other in their entirety,— all that is left of them. General Meade has at last concentrated his forces; Lee has accomplished the same; and they are ready for the closing struggle. Such was the order of joining battle, at Gettysburg, on the morning of the third day.

CHAPTER VII

THE MEETING OF THE WAYS

BEAUTIFUL for situation is Gettysburg, fairest among the cities of the Keystone State, far-famed and most glorious of battlefields! City of monuments, adorned in the fair garments of Peace, environed with the memorials of war. On every hand are the open pages whereon Heroism and Patriotism have written their deeds of valour and endurance, in lines so deep that Time himself shall not efface their memory.

Gettysburg stands in an undulating valley. A half-mile to the east the sparkling waters of Rock Creek meander away southward until lost in over-shadowing woods that darken the rocky slopes of bold Culp's Hill.

Northward the fair, cultivated valley, with its wealth of garden, field, orchard, and meadow, stretches afar. To the west, seven hundred yards away, the Lutheran Theological Seminary crowns

the summit of Seminary Ridge, which extends in a
north and south direction as far as the eye can reach.
From Seminary Ridge westward for a thousand
yards or more the country slopes away in undulating
waves to Willoughby Run.

South of the city, like the hanging gardens of
Babylon of old, rises Cemetery Hill, beautifully
adorned to its summit with spreading trees and
towering monuments. Cemetery Hill is prolonged
to the eastward, separated only by a grassy depres-
sion from the rocky ridge known as Culp's Hill,
which rises to an almost impregnable citadel and
then slopes away to the southeastward more gently
though still rugged, for a mile or more to Rock
Creek. Cemetery Hill is also prolonged to the
southwestward by what is called the Emmetsburg
Road Ridge, until it intersects and becomes a part
of the Seminary Ridge, two and a half miles away.
Still another ridge puts out from Cemetery Hill to
the southward, which rises very gently from the
valley to the westward at first, becoming more
prominent with the distance, and two miles and a
half to the southward terminates in Round Top,

the glory of the Gettysburg hills, overlooking all
the surrounding landscape. Southward from Round
Top the valley of Rock Creek spreads out in its
loveliness, beyond the ken of human vision.

A dozen highways lead into and converge at
Gettysburg, and they were all there in 1863. Across
the streams, along the ridges, threading the valleys,
over the hills they came, from the north, from the
south, from the east, and from the west; and it was
owing to the fact that Gettysburg stood in 1863, as
she still stands to-day, at the "meeting of the ways,"
that she was destined to become the central point in,
and thus to give her name to, the pivotal battle of
America's civil war.

Beginning at the west, or a little north of west,
where the battle began, there is first, the Chambersburg Pike, which crosses Willoughby Run a mile
and a half away, and Seminary Ridge, seven or
eight hundred yards north of west from the city.
Just north of this road and only a short distance
from it is the railroad from Hagerstown, that cuts
the line of monuments demarcating the old battle-
line, just east of Willoughby Run. At the time of

the battle the railroad was not there, but the grading for it had been begun, and a deep cut ran through Seminary Ridge, wherein now runs the railroad. Second, the Mummasburg Road from the northwest, crossing Willoughby Run and Seminary Ridge at a somewhat greater distance from the city than the first; third and fourth, the Carlisle and Newville Roads, which unite about a mile north of the city and enter it as the Carlisle Road; fifth, the Harrisburg Road from the capital of the State, which approaches and enters the city from east of north, crossing Rock Creek about a mile out; sixth and seventh, the York Pike and the Hunterstown Road, which, uniting just before crossing Rock Creek about three-fourths of a mile northeastward, enter the city as the York Pike. Upon these seven roads the various corps, divisions, and brigades comprising Lee's army of invasion concentrated at Gettysburg to meet the Army of the Potomac.

Then from the eastward there is the Hanover Road, not used by either army until the third of July, when Stuart's Confederate cavalry moved out thereon at an early hour in the morning of that day, and a mile or two east of Gettysburg was met and defeated by Pleasonton's Union cavalry. The Hanover Road crosses Rock Creek about half a mile directly east of the city.

From the southward there are three roads: first, the Baltimore Pike, which crosses Rock Creek three or four miles to the southeast of the city and enters it over the eastern slope of Cemetery Hill; second, the Taneytown Road, leading up directly from the southward and just east of Round Top and the southern prolongation of Cemetery Ridge, and entering the city over and along the western slope of Cemetery Hill; third, the Emmetsburg Road from the southwest following along the crest of the Emmetsburg Road Ridge, crossing the Taneytown Road, and intersecting the Baltimore Pike on the northern slope of Cemetery Hill in the outskirts of the city, thus forming her main street north and south, called Baltimore Street. Upon the aforesaid three roads the various corps, divisions, and brigades of the Union army concentrated at Gettysburg to give battle to Lee's Army of Northern Virginia. There was one other road from the southwest called

the Hagerstown or Fairfield Road, which crosses
Willoughby Run something like a mile and a half
south of west, and Seminary Ridge a half-mile
directly west of Gettysburg. This road was not
used by either army before or during the battle, but
it led away from Gettysburg through the South
Mountain passes to Hagerstown and the Potomac
River; and during the battle Lee guarded this road
as the apple of his eye, for it represented his back-
door of escape if the battle went against him. After
the battle was over he found this gateway through
the mountains a most convenient and important
way over which to lead his defeated army back to
the shelter of his friendly Virginian hills beyond
the Potomac River, and he neglected not to make
good use of it for that purpose.

CHAPTER VIII

WHEN dawned the morning of July first, General Buford occupied this unique position: With one small division of cavalry numbering about three thousand men, he was guarding the crossings of Willoughby Run on two highways leading into, and from a mile and a half to a mile and three-fourths northwest of, Gettysburg; Lee's whole army was from four to twenty-three miles away, every division and brigade of which was marching steadily and rapidly toward him; only two corps of the Union army were in position to support him, one of them numbering 8,500 men (Stannard's brigade of the third division not being with the First Corps in the first day's battle) being six miles away, and the other (the Eleventh Corps) 9,500 strong, at Emmetsburg, thirteen miles distant; while the balance of the Army of the Potomac and the commanding General thereof were far out of reach for that day, and in blissful ignorance of his situation. But Buford quailed not; and Heth, with the leading division of Lee's army, found him at his post. The Eighth Illinois Cavalry of Gamble's brigade, out on the Chambersburg Pike about a mile west of Willoughby Run, opened the battle with Archer's brigade of Heth's infantry, about eight o'clock in the morning. The First Corps of the Union army was early astir, and as we were marching along the Emmetsburg Road in the direction of Gettysburg, our ears were saluted with the first cannon-shot of the opening battle. The shots sounded far away, and we had no idea that we were coming almost immediately into the presence of the enemy. We were within a mile of Gettysburg and could see the fair city to the northeastward, reposing in peace that summer morning ere the battle began that was to shake the very stones of her foundations.

It was just before nine o'clock, and here we were met by General Reynolds, who had returned to urge us forward with all possible speed to the support of Buford. General Reynolds sat upon his horse on the west side of the highway facing us, and as we marched near the head of the column we had a fair view of his features. The General looked careworn, and we thought, very sad, but the high purpose of his patriotic soul was stamped upon every lineament. It was the last time we saw him. He directed the turning of our column to the westward and then rode rapidly toward Gettysburg to confer with Buford at his headquarters at the Seminary. Within a short half-hour thereafter he had given his life for his country.

As we turned from the Emmetsburg Road westward, scattering solid-shot tore through the tree-tops above our heads, reminding us that the battle was on in earnest, and much nearer than we had supposed. Then Fairchild, our Colonel, sprang from his horse, which he gave to the care of Sanford, his hostler, as he shouted his command, "Non-combatants to the rear!" We marched rapidly forward, loading our guns as we advanced. Within five hundred yards from the point where our Colonel dismounted we reached the crest of Seminary Ridge. Five hundred yards farther, and we entered the edge of McPherson's Woods — afterwards called

Reynolds' Woods — on the crest of a second ridge, where Buford's thin line was heroically holding Archer's infantry in check, which was advancing steadily through the woods from the westward.

At the Battle of Gettysburg, and long before, " all quality, pride, pomp, and circumstance of glorious war" had disappeared from the American armies on either side. A few regiments or brigades wore some distinguishing feature of dress besides the corps-badge, by which they were recognized, but there was to be seen among our embattled ranks nothing to compare with the pomp and show of war, as portrayed by Hugo, on the field of Waterloo:

" The flaming calbacks, the waving sabre-taches, the crossed shoulder-belts, the grenade cartridge-boxes, the dolmans of the huzzars, the red boots with a thousand creases, the heavy shakos festooned with fringe, the almost black infantry of Brunswick united with the scarlet infantry of England, the English soldiers with great white circular pads on their sleeves for epaulets, the Hanoverian light horse with their oblong leather caps with copper bands and flowing plumes of red horsehair, the Scotch with bare knees and plaids, and the large white gaiters of our grenadiers."

In our whole army there was no more distinguished brigade in the matter of dress than the old Iron Brigade of the First Corps, which was the first infantry of the Army of the Potomac to relieve the cavalry and join battle with Heth's leading brigade of Lee's infantry on the morning of the first of July. This distinguishing feature of dress was not for style or foolishness, but simply because the brigade at its first organization had been supplied with the black regulation army-hats instead of caps, which articles of headgear were retained throughout the war. These hats were looped up on the right side, and contained a small plume or feather, also on the right side, and a blue cord for a band. This brigade was known throughout both armies as the " Black Hats "; but even these hats were far from showy when the old brigade relieved the cavalry that morning. At this stage of the game the regiments of the Army of the Potomac were not there for vain-glory, but for business; and the same may be truthfully said of the Confederates. What we saw that July morning as we neared the edge of the woods was a thin line of horsemen dressed in faded blue with yellow trimmings, powder-begrimed and disordered by the heat of battle, fighting as best they could to delay the advancing enemy. Then came the order, "Forward into line," and the Second Wisconsin Infantry, number- ing about three full companies, surged forward like a wave of the sea, and a dark line of worn and ragged blue swept on toward the wooded crest. Behind that line the cavalry retired, and on the crest of the hill we were confronted by a heavy line of ragged butternut, firing steadily as they advanced up the slope. Before us was the far-extending line of Archer's brigade; behind us were three regiments of our own brigade, which, wave after wave, surged forward to extend our line to the right and to the left, as we moved steadily down the slope receiving a galling fire from Archer's men. It was, as in thousands of other instances, just the unadorned, long-drawn-out line of ragged, dirty blue against the long-drawn-out line of dirty, ragged butternut, with no "pomp of war" about it, and no show or style except our old black hats. Archer's men recognized these at once, and shouted to each other, "Thar comes them old black-hats! It's the Army of the Potomac, sure!"

GETTYSBURG

Before we had advanced thirty yards into the woods, our Colonel received a severe wound, from which he lost an arm; and immediately after, our Lieutenant-Colonel was killed. We held our fire until within ten yards of the Confederate line, and then gave them a volley that counted; for Archer's line gave way, retreating slowly and stubbornly through the woods and finally across Willoughby Run. We followed closely upon their heels, and, crossing the run about a moment later, captured General Archer and several hundred of his men who had taken shelter behind a clump of willows. In the charge across the Run this willow-clump, very compact and interwoven, divided the second regiment into two parts, our veteran being in the right battalion or division. The left division was led by Captain Charles Dow, and to him General Archer surrendered and offered his sword. But Captain Dow replied: "Keep your sword, General, and go to the rear; one sword is all I need on this line." So General Archer passed in front of the willow-clump toward our right before crossing the Run to the rear. When within about forty yards of us he was met by a lieutenant of the second regiment then serving as a staff officer, who demanded of Archer his sword. At first the General refused, trying to explain his right to retain it by the order of Captain Dow, but the lieutenant insisted, and to save further trouble the General surrendered his sword to the man who had no right to receive it. It is not always that the man on the outmost line receives the reward which is his due.

Just as General Archer and his captured men were crossing the Run to the rear, under a hastily improvised guard, and it became certain that we had won the first heat of battle, a sergeant of our company, Jonathan Bryan by name, was shot through the heart by a Confederate from the edge of the woods beyond a field in our front, while waving his hat and cheering for victory. He was by birth a Pennsylvanian, and one of the best and bravest among the soldiers of the Second Wisconsin. Comrade Bryan was the only man of our regiment killed west of Willoughby Run.

When the old veteran visited Gettysburg in 1900, he found no stone marking the spot where the brave

common-soldier fell, nor yet a monument or marker
to show the place where we captured Archer, nor
a line on our regimental monument telling to the
world the important fact in the history of the regiment, that the Second Wisconsin Infantry crossed
Willoughby Run on the first day of July, 1863, and
there captured General Archer of the Confederate
army. Why this oversight or neglect?

A few moments after comrade Bryan was killed,
our line was withdrawn to the east side, and we took
up a defensive position with Willoughby Run in
our front at close rifle-range. Our brigade comprised five regiments, but the Sixth Wisconsin,
being on division rear-guard during the march of
the morning, was not with us. It followed the
second brigade, coming upon the field a little later,
and with that brigade it passed by our rear and
engaged in the morning's first battle with Davis's
Confederates, who were also of Heth's division
farther to the right, extending our battle-line beyond
or north of the Chambersburg Pike.

Immediately after forming our battle-line east of
Willoughby Run, we threw out a skirmish or picket

line well screened by the bushes on the bank of the Run, and then proceeded to call the roll of companies and take an inventory of our losses. We went into that morning skirmish with a total strength of three hundred and two men in our regiment. The battle did not last more than thirty minutes, but our loss in killed and wounded was one hundred and sixteen, or thirty-eight per cent. This fact shows, as heretofore stated, that the Confederate soldiers were expert marksmen and used good powder. The other regiments of our brigade did not meet with so heavy a loss, for the Confederate fire was concentrated upon us, as we charged down the slope through the grove; but their prompt and active support enabled us to drive General Archer to cover, and, as Longstreet tells us in his "Memoirs," page 354, "captured General Archer and one thousand of Heth's men." Herein Longstreet gives us greater credit than belongs to us, a generosity unusual for him. We captured Archer and more men than the second regiment took into battle; but our brigade did not capture a thousand at that time, though during the whole day the two brigades of Wadsworth's division captured a thousand or more of Heth's men. Our second brigade — Cutler's — was also victorious on our right; and between the two we humbled the pride of Archer's and Davis's brigades, thoroughly.

Following this sharp skirmish of the morning, there was a lull in the battle, lasting from half to three-fourths of an hour. The second and third divisions of the First Corps arrived during the lull and extended our lines to the right and left, making the battle-front of the First Corps a mile or more in length, facing nearly westward, and in that line we mustered 8,500 men, before our losses of the morning, which were severe.

Buford's cavalry, which had fought Heth's infantry for an hour before being relieved by our First Corps, and had lost heavily in the engagement, then moved to the northward to protect our right. On the other hand, the Confederates, under A. P. Hill commanding their Third Corps, were re-forming their lines for the renewal of the battle. Archer's brigade was commanded by Colonel Fry, and reinforced with Pettigrew's and Brockenbrough's brigades. Hill was also reinforced by Pender's division; Thomas's brigade on his left supporting Davis, and Lane's, Scales', and Perrins' brigades supporting his right and overlapping the Union left. This gave the Confederates' strength in our front at eight brigades, as against our six, each of which was numerically stronger than ours.

While we lay in battle-line during this lull, our wounded were assisted to the rear, but the dead were left where they fell, — in fact we had no men to spare from our ranks for any purpose where the absolute necessity did not exist; and we noticed a soldier of our company who had been wounded, some distance to the rear, as we came through the wood. He had secured two muskets from the field, which he was using as crutches, and when we last saw him he was far up the slope, making his way off the field without assistance, though so severely wounded that his leg was afterwards amputated above the knee. He lived for many years after the war ended.

Before the battle reopened, word was passed along our line informing us of the death of General

Reynolds. He was killed a few moments after he went into action in the morning, a little to the right and about fifty yards in front of the point where we entered the wood. A granite monument marks the spot where he fell, and the grove is now renamed " Reynolds' Woods."

About half-past ten o'clock our pickets reported the advancing of the enemy in strong force, and soon thereafter the battle reopened all along the line.

In the immediate front of the position held by the Second Wisconsin in the wood, Willoughby Run ran in and out among the willow-clumps, leaving many rocky spaces free from cover; and as the Confederates advanced to cross the Run, we tried to make it lively for them, and so far succeeded that they were a full hour in forcing the passage; but they were brave and determined, and after desperate resistance we were obliged to concede them the privilege of crossing. However, we did not then surrender the grove, but held on to it for hours, yielding it only foot by foot, and inch by inch. The grove was our citadel, and it in itself furnished the means of strong defence. Every tree was a breastwork, every log a barricade, every bush a cover and concealment, and we made good use of every defensive object.

From Willoughby Run to Seminary Ridge the distance is not great. It is 475 yards from the creek to the ridge at the eastern edge of the woods, where our battle with Archer began in the morning; and 500 yards from the edge of the grove to the crest of Seminary Ridge. We measured this ground carefully in 1900, because we remembered it as a good long two miles in that day of battle. The whole distance is less than a thousand yards, but it took Hill's Confederates five weary hours to travel it, and then they did not quite reach the goal of their ambition until after we had abandoned it from other causes.

CHAPTER IX

HOWARD IN COMMAND

WHILE this struggle in Reynolds' Grove was going on in all its fury, and the battle was raging desperately along the whole front of the First Corps, General Howard arrived in advance of his Corps (the Eleventh) and assumed command of the field as the ranking General. The cupola of the Lutheran Seminary was the headquarters of the Union forces on the first day of July, 1863, first under Buford and Reynolds, later under Doubleday, and finally under Howard. The cupola was a tower of observation from which all the surrounding country could be seen as from no other point; from that cupola General Howard caught his first full view of the battlefield and the situation, and at once resolved to do his utmost in fighting to a successful finish the mighty game that Buford and Reynolds had so heroically begun. He therefore directed the first and third divisions of the

GETTYSBURG

Eleventh Corps, under General Carl Schurz, to extend our right from the Mummasburg Road, where it crosses the Seminary Ridge about three-fourths of a mile northwest of Gettysburg, eastward to Rock Creek; and he placed the second division in reserve on Cemetery Hill, south of the city, knowing that it would become necessary to retire to that position before reinforcements could arrive. This was a wise and soldier-like movement on the part of General Howard, as was afterwards demonstrated.

Schurz's two divisions gave us an additional strength of four brigades, or 6,300 men, swelling our aggregate battle strength to 17,800 including Buford's cavalry.

Later, Steinwehr was ordered to send Coster's brigade to protect Schurz's right, on Rock Creek northeast from Gettysburg. Counting the full strength of the Eleventh Corps in the day's battle, Howard's force comprised about 21,000 men. Schurz's line of battle from Seminary Ridge to Rock Creek was about three-fourths of a mile in length, and formed nearly a right angle with the line of the First Corps. As Schurz advanced his line northward he was met by Ewell's third division, commanded by Rodes, comprising the brigades of Daniel, Iverson, Doles, Ramseur, and O'Neal, five brigades in all against Schurz's four brigades. Rodes had also occupied Seminary Ridge north of the Mummasburg Road, and placing his artillery in position on Oak Hill, a prominent point of Seminary Ridge, about a half-mile northward, used it with deadly effect both on Doubleday's right and Schurz's left, while the latter was forming his brigades for battle.

As thus extended by the forces of Schurz against Rodes, the battle was in full progress from Seminary Ridge to Rock Creek by half-past one or two o'clock, and all that afternoon raged in great fury on both of Howard's battle-fronts; to the westward under Doubleday, and to the northward under Schurz.

Out on the west front, we of the Iron Brigade, after hours of desperate fighting, had at last been driven from Reynolds' Grove, about three o'clock P.M., and our lines to the right and left seemed to be giving way. When we found ourselves on the eastern verge of the wood there was behind us an open field extending to the crest of Seminary Ridge, five hundred yards distant. To our right and to our left our line bent back toward the ridge, and our flanks would soon be exposed; besides, we had more than we could do to hold our front. After abandoning the grove there was but one other position short of Seminary Ridge that there was any chance of holding. That was in the hollow, — a kind of dry run or wet weather creek between the two ridges, two hundred and fifty yards from either. This position we held for some time, giving the Johnnies a hot reception as they came out of the wood and advanced down the slope.

Behind us on the ridge was our artillery, which up to this time had given us no assistance in the battle. In fact it had been an infantry engagement along our part of the line since the opening of the battle in the morning. Not an artillery shot, not a bursting shell, not a swish of canister had disturbed our lines that we can now remember. It was, or had been, peculiarly an infantry battle, and on both sides the artillery had kept hands off, or had been engaged in other parts of the field. But when the butternut line surged heavily down the slope upon us, and we saw to the right and the left that we were still in advance of our general lines, and the hollow became hot with the incessant hum of the bees of battle, then we concluded that we must make a dash for the crest of the hill, where the artillery could assist us. We cannot remember of hearing any order to retreat, but as a flock of birds are seen to quit their tree at the same instant, so every man seemed to take in at a glance the necessity of hastily withdrawing. If our recollection is not at fault, we passed over that last two hundred and fifty yards much more rapidly than over any other portion of our journey from Willoughby Run to Seminary Ridge on the first day of July, 1863.

The Confederates were surging down the opposite slope under a cloud of fire and smoke, when we started to gain the ridge, and immediately they divined our intention. They seemed to think it would be the proper thing for them to run in under the cover of our batteries with us, and they did their very best to accomplish that strategy. It became at once a life and death race for all of us. Any man left on the face of that hillside when the artillery should open with canister would never fight again. It was certain death to any comrade disabled in that wild rush; a wound, a slip of the foot, a misstep, were fatal.

The Confederates had ceased firing and were giving their whole attention to the race, for, blue or gray, we must get inside the range of those gaping mouths before they belch their fire, or we are doomed. How many of our comrades were left behind in that awful race, God only knows! We who got in had time to take one hasty glance behind. Our boys seemed safe; there were a few of them in a kind of fringe hanging between the battery sections, that the gunners were swerving their pieces to avoid, but farther down, two-thirds of the way up the hill, came the Confederates, yelling like demons, in a mad charge for our guns.

We had struck the crest just north of a small building which stood near the north end of the Seminary and about forty yards south of the Chambersburg Pike. Here was stationed one section of Stevens' Fifth Maine Battery, the other sections being stationed, one between this small building and the Seminary, and the other south of the Seminary. Across the Chambersburg Pike were stationed three guns of Battery B, Fourth United States Artillery, in half battery, the other half battery being stationed a hundred yards farther north and beyond the railroad cut. Along the ridge north and south of these batteries, which were in our immediate vicinity, were ranged the other batteries of the First Corps, namely, Battery L, First New York, Battery B, First Pennsylvania, and Battery B, Second Maine; five batteries, or thirty guns in all. These guns were brimmed with shell or double-shotted with canister; they were carefully posted by the best field artillerymen in the army; every man was at his station, and they were awaiting this very opportunity. The charging Confederates were brave men, — in fact, no braver ever faced death in any cause, and none ever faced more certain death!

Almost at the same moment, as if every lanyard was pulled by the same hand, this line of artillery opened, and Seminary Ridge blazed with a solid sheet of flame, and the missiles of death that swept its western slopes no human beings could endure. After a few moments of the belching of the artillery, the blinding smoke shut out the sun and obstructed the view. We of the infantry fell into line between the artillery sections and assisted with our musketry, keeping up the fire until our pieces grew hot in our hands, and the darkness, as of night, had settled upon us. Not a Confederate reached our line. After we had ceased firing and the smoke of battle had lifted, we looked again, but the charging Confederates were not there. Only the dead and dying remained on the bloody slopes of Seminary Ridge.

This struggle for the possession of Seminary Ridge is described by one of the boys of Battery B of the Fourth United States Artillery, whose station was about seventy yards north of our position, who gives an account of the same battle from an artilleryman's point of view, and also from a different but near-by position. The " Cannoneer " writes of this battle as follows:

GETTYSBURG

" In the meantime our infantry out in the field toward the creek was being slowly but surely overpowered, and our lines were being forced in toward the Seminary. It was now considerably past noon. In addition to the struggle going on in our immediate front, the sounds of a heavy attack from the north side were heard, and away out beyond the creek to the south a strong force could be seen advancing and overlapping our left. The enemy was coming nearer, both in front and on the north, and stray balls began to zip and whistle around our ears with unpleasant frequency. Then we saw the batteries that had been holding the position in advance of us limber up and fall back toward the Seminary, and the enemy simultaneously advance his batteries down the road. All our infantry out toward the creek on both sides of the pike began to fall back.

" The enemy did not press them very closely, but halted for nearly an hour to re-form his lines, which had been very much shattered by the battle of the forenoon. At last, having re-formed his lines behind the low ridges in his front, he made his appearance in grand shape. His line stretched from the railroad grading across the Cashtown or Chambersburg Pike, and through the fields south of it half way to the Fairfield Road — nearly a mile in length. First we could see the tips of their color-staffs coming up over the little ridge, then the points of their bayonets, and then the Johnnies themselves, coming on with a steady tramp, tramp, and with loud yells. It was now apparent that our old Battery's turn had come again, and the embattled boys who stood so grimly at their posts felt that another page must be added to the record of Buena Vista and Antietam. The term ' boys ' is literally true, because of our gun detachment alone, consisting of a sergeant, two corporals, seven cannoneers, and six drivers, only four had hair on their faces; while the other twelve were beardless boys whose age would not average nineteen years, and who, at

any other period of our history, would have been at school.
The same was more or less true of all the other gun detachments.*

"But if boys in years, they were veterans in battle, and braver or steadier soldiers than they were never faced a foe.

"A glance along our line at that moment would have afforded a rare study for an artist. As the day was hot, many had their jackets off, some with sleeves rolled up, and they exchanged little words of cheer with each other as the gray line came on. In quick, sharp tones, like successive reports of a repeating rifle, came Davison's orders:

"'Load — Canister — Double!' There was a hustling of cannoneers, a few thumps of the rammer-heads, and then: 'Ready — By piece — At will — Fire!'

"We were formed 'straddle' of the railroad cut, the 'Old Man,' as we called Captain Stewart, with three guns forming the right half-battery on the north side, and Davison with the three guns of the left half on the south side. Stewart's three guns were somewhat in advance of ours, forming a slight *échelon* in half-battery, while our three guns were in open order, bringing the left gun close to the Chambersburg Road. We were formed in a small field, and our guns raked the road to the top of the low crest forming the east bank of Willoughby Run. The time of day was about 2:30 or 3 P.M. Hall's and Reynolds' batteries which had held the crest in our right-front had retired to Seminary Ridge, and all the infantry of the First Corps that had been fighting in our front had fallen back. Directly in our front — that is to say, on both sides of the pike — the Rebel infantry, whose left lapped the north side of the pike quite up to the line of the railroad grading, had been forced to halt and lie down to avoid the tornado of canister that we had given them from the moment

---

*This was true of our whole army: an army of *boys*.

GETTYSBURG

they came in sight over the bank of the creek. But the regiments in the field to their right, south of the pike, kept on, swinging their right flanks forward as if to take us in reverse, or cut us off from the rest of our troops near the Seminary. At this moment, Davison, bleeding from two desperate wounds and so weak that one of the boys had to hold him up on his feet — one ankle being shattered — ordered us to form the half-battery action left, by wheeling on the left gun as a pivot, so as to bring the half-battery on a line with the Chambersburg Pike, muzzles facing south. His object was to rake the front of the Rebel line closing in on us from that side. Of the four men left at our gun when this order was given, two had bloody heads, but they were still fighting, and Sergeant Mitchel jumped on our off wheel to help us. This change of front gave us a clear rake along the Rebel line for a whole brigade length, but it exposed our right flank to the raking volleys of their infantry near the pike, who at that moment began to get up and come on again. Then for seven or eight minutes ensued probably the most desperate fighting ever waged between artillery and infantry at close range, without a particle of cover on either side. They gave us volley after volley in front and flank, and we gave them double-canister as fast as we could load. The Sixth Wisconsin and the Eleventh Pennsylvania infantry crawled up over the bank of the railroad cut, or behind the rail fence in rear of Stewart's caissons, and joined their musketry to our canister, while from the north side of the cut flashed the chain-lightning of the ' Old Man's ' half-battery in one solid streak.

" At this time our left half-battery, taking their first line *en écharpe*, swept it so clean with double-canister that they sagged away from the road to get cover from the fences and trees that lined it. From our second round on, a gray squirrel could not have crossed that road alive. The very guns became things of life — not implements, but comrades.

[84]

GETTYSBURG

Every man was doing the work of two or three. At our gun, at the finish, there were only the Corporal, No. 1, and No. 3, with two drivers fetching water. The water in their buckets was like ink, their faces and hands smeared all over with burnt powder. The thumbstall of No. 3 was burned to a crisp by the hot ventfield. Between the black of the burnt powder and the crimson streaks of his bloody head, Corporal Packard looked like a demon from below. Up and down the line, men reeling and falling; splinters flying from wheels and axles, where bullets hit; in rear, horses tearing and plunging, mad with wounds or terror; drivers yelling; shells bursting; shot shrieking overhead, howling about our ears, or throwing up great clouds of dust where they struck; the musketry crashing on three sides of us; all crash on crash, and peal on peal; smoke, dust, splinters, blood, wreck, and carnage indescribable; but the brass guns of old B still bellowed, and not a man or boy flinched or faltered!"

Such was the battle as seen and experienced by the artillery; and all along that line, whether of artillery or infantry, the first of July, 1863, was a day long to be remembered.

CHAPTER X

IN the eyes of an American soldier, perhaps in the eyes of any soldier, there is nothing so beautiful and inspiring as the flag under which he has fought long and earnestly, when it shines out triumphantly above a hard-won battlefield. His best girl's picture that he wears against his heart, and is mindful to snatch a glimpse of at the first opportunity after the battle is over, is not more beautiful. Even the old veteran's silver-haired wife, faithful and true for a lifetime, is not more inspiring to look upon in his old age, than was the flag victorious in the days of his youth.

So, when the clouds lifted and floated away from Seminary Ridge that July afternoon and we saw the Stars and Stripes — up to that moment more frequently the emblem of defeat than of victory for us — emerging, all glorious, from the smoke of battle in the fulness of victory, as we hoped, can you wonder, O reader, that Old Glory appeared surpassingly beautiful to us on that occasion? The flag our fathers gave us is the emblem of our country, representing liberty, justice, and humanity, and in time of war, right or wrong, it is every American soldier's duty to honour and defend it against all enemies, with his last breath and last drop of blood; but in time of peace it is the duty of every American citizen to see to it that the flag of free America shall remain the emblem of liberty, justice, and humanity, to the end that her soldiers may fail not in the possession of the spirit of patriotism, so necessary in war, yielding not to adversity, nor becoming disheartened by defeat.

In those dark days of the Civil War, the Union soldier, true to his patriotic convictions, saw victory beyond defeat, and beyond victory a triumphant peace, that surely and certainly would crown his efforts at last. Therefore at Gettysburg we hailed that dear old flag, shining out for a few brief moments above Seminary Ridge, as the harbinger of victory and peace. Then we looked hastily for the proof of our hopes. In our front there was no sign of the enemy between our position and Reynolds' Grove, but to the right and to the left the smoke of battle still enshrouded all distant points.

Company H of the Second Wisconsin was then the colour company of the regiment; and as we stood on the ridge watching the movement of events, Captain Nat Rollins called us around the old regimental flag, which, riddled and rent, was held proudly in its place by Sergeant Davison, informing us that it was Major Mansfield's order that the whole company — reduced to a handful of men — should act as colour guard. The Captain, looking at his watch, said, "It is four o'clock." What further he would have said was cut short by some one shouting, "Look there! What troops are those?" pointing away to the northeast. We all looked, of course, and we saw the whole valley north of the city, from Seminary Ridge on the west to Rock Creek on the east, alive with rapidly advancing troops, bearing triumphantly above them the saucy battle-flags of the Confederacy, and we knew that Schurz's line had been driven from its position. Still nearer, in the outskirts of the city, we caught a glimpse of the

Stars and Stripes disappearing behind the walls and buildings, borne on by our troops, retiring in haste and confusion. Any flag should appear beautiful and inspiring to those who follow and defend it, according to what it represents to them; but that line of Confederate battle-flags, though representing disunion, at that moment presented a stronger guaranty of victory for the Confederacy on the field of Gettysburg than the Stars and Stripes seeking cover from the northward, or ranged along the crest of Seminary Ridge, presented in behalf of the Union.

The cause of this sudden change in our view of the situation was the fact that about an hour before, Early's division of Ewell's corps, coming in from the northeast along the York Road, had crossed Rock Creek close up to the city, driving his four brigades, like a huge wedge, between the flank and rear of Barlow's Union division resting its right on Rock Creek, and Coster's brigade, sent from Steinwehr's reserve on Cemetery Hill to protect the Union flank at the point where the York Road crosses the creek. Schurz's brigades were then hotly engaged with Rodes' five brigades along their whole front; and the four additional brigades of Early's division, swelling the Confederate strength to nine brigades, as against the six brigades of the Eleventh Corps, swept Coster back toward Cemetery Hill, and then threw their full strength against Schurz's right and rear. Thus assailed in front and flank, Schurz's two divisions holding our north front were rolled up and swept from the field. And that was what we saw, in its closing stages, as we turned our eyes northeastward from Seminary Ridge at four o'clock, and scanned the valley north of Gettysburg.

Of that event let General Gordon tell; he commanded one of Early's brigades and was on that part of the field:

" Returning from the banks of the Susquehanna, and meeting at Gettysburg, July first, 1863, the advance of Lee's forces, my command was thrown quickly and squarely on the right flank of the Union army. A more timely arrival never occurred. The battle had been raging for four or five hours. The Confederate General, Archer, with a large portion of his brigade, had been captured. Heth and Scales, Confederate Generals, had been wounded. The ranking Union commander on the field, General Reynolds, had been killed, and Howard assigned to the command. The battle, upon the issue of which hung, perhaps, the fate of the Confederacy, was in full blast. The Union forces were advancing and pressing back Lee's left, and threatening to envelop it. The Confederates were stubbornly contesting every foot of ground, but the Southern left was slowly yielding. A few moments more, and the day's battle might have been ended by the complete turning of Lee's flank. I was ordered to move at once to the aid of the heavily pressed Confederates. With a ringing yell my command rushed upon the line posted to protect the Union right. Here a hand-to-hand struggle occurred. That protecting Union line once broken, left my command not only on their right flank, but obliquely in rear of it. Any troops that were ever marshalled would, under like conditions, have been as surely and swiftly shattered. There was no alternative for Howard's men except to break and fly, or to throw down their arms and surrender. Under the concentrated fire from the front and flank, the marvel is that any escaped. . . .

" The whole of that portion of the Union army in my front was in inextricable confusion and in flight. They were necessarily in flight, for my troops were upon their flank and rapidly sweeping down the lines. The firing upon my men had almost ceased. Large bodies of the Union troops were throwing down their arms and surrendering, because in disorganized and confused masses, they were wholly powerless either to check the movement or return the fire.

" As far down the lines as my eye could reach, the Union troops were in retreat. Those at a distance were still resisting, but giving ground, and it was only necessary for me to press forward in order to insure the same results which invariably follow such flank movements."

In the foregoing account General Gordon takes much credit to his command, and the reader might readily receive the impression that Gordon, and not Early, commanded the Confederate division thrown so effectively upon Howard's right flank at that time; but otherwise Gordon's description, as we saw the field from Seminary Ridge, is impressingly accurate. There was no doubt in the mind of any of us who saw the action as to the true condition of affairs. Looking closer, we saw that the retreat from our own line farther to the westward had already begun, and must have been in progress for some time, as the Chambersburg Pike all the way from Seminary Ridge to the city was black with our troops in swift retreat. To our brigade no order for retreat was given that we can remember. In fact there was no time to waste; so we stood not on the order of our going, but went at once.

From our position Gettysburg was seven hundred yards southeast of us (we have since measured the distance), and the Chambersburg Pike, which ran along our right and rear, was wide and smooth and down grade all the way, and we made good use of it. The artillery had the right of way by virtue of their power to possess it, and they drove their horses at a pace that would have surprised Jehu, the mad driver of old.

General Doubleday, who commanded our First Corps, in his written account of this retreat, says: " I waited until the artillery had gone, and then rode back to the town with my staff. As we passed through the streets, pale and frightened women came out and offered us coffee and food, and implored us not to abandon them. . . . The First Corps was broken and defeated, but not dismayed. There were but few left, but they showed the true spirit of soldiers. They walked leisurely from the Seminary to the town, and did not run."

It would be interesting to one old veteran to know when the retreat began as heretofore spoken of, or where General Doubleday " waited until the artillery had gone." We of the Black Hat Brigade did not wait a second after taking in at a glance the full peril of our situation, but dashed down the Chambersburg Pike. While we were running our very best, Stevens' Fifth Maine Battery, that we defended or that defended us while we were repulsing the Confederates' last charge on Seminary

Ridge, and which we had left in position — knowing well the ability of the artillery to get out of there faster than we could — and also Battery B of the Fourth U. S. passed us, their horses on a full run, and the cannoneers clinging to the caissons and limber chests; but we saw nothing of General Doubleday and his staff waiting in the fence-corners along the pike.

Of course it stirs the heart of an old veteran to have his General speak in words of commendation of himself and comrades; nevertheless, we must conclude that a number of us left Seminary Ridge some time after our General, for when we arrived in the city, there were no " pale and frightened women on the streets," with coffee and cookies for us. They had exhausted their supply before our arrival and had gone into their houses, as any sensible lady would have done about that time and under the same circumstances. In fact the streets were not the places for women then. It was all right and a good thing for the First Corps and the army, that General Doubleday did not remain too long on Seminary Ridge, nor in the city, for he was a good soldier, and the army and the country needed his services; but it is one of the facts of history that we lost in prisoners taken by the enemy that first day of July from the First and Eleventh Corps, about 2,500 men, most of them captured on that retreat and in the city, after General Doubleday had ridden through and out of it.

The boys said afterwards that they got tangled up in the names of the brigade commanders of Schurz's third division of the Eleventh Corps, General Von Schimmelfennig and Colonel Krzyzanowski. These officers were from the *Vaterland,* or from some other foreign country, and they had brought their own names with them. As General Von Schimmelfennig commanded the third division when Schurz took command of the Eleventh Corps, there really was some cause for the entanglement in the streets of Gettysburg in addition to Early's flank movement; and the soldiers will have their jokes. We were surely greatly hurried and badly tangled in the streets of Gettysburg on that retreat, however, and many a brave Union soldier went to Richmond and to his death on that account.

When we reached the city the Confederates were already in possession of the northern and eastern portions of it. Generals Howard, Doubleday, and Schurz were then on Cemetery Hill, where they should have been, re-forming their shattered commands to meet Lee's expected attack on their new position that afternoon, and long before the sun went down; but had they, or any of them, taken the precaution to plant a few pieces of artillery in positions to sweep the streets of Gettysburg, supported by detachments of infantry under officers with staying qualities, to cover our retreat, many of our men might have been saved from captivity, who, conditions being otherwise, were lost. The fact is, that our generals as well as ourselves were badly tangled.

When we reached the city the Confederates were having everything their own way. Those of us who could run the gantlet rejoined our commands and rallied on Cemetery Hill, and those who could not, but were cut off and picked up by the Confederates, went to Richmond. It was 4:30 o'clock P.M., and the battle and retreat of July first were over.

CHAPTER XI

LEE arrived on the field of Gettysburg, prob-. ably about four o'clock of July first. He was, says Longstreet, "in time to view the closing operations of the engagement. His headquarters were on Seminary Ridge at the crossing of the Cashtown or Chambersburg Road. After surveying the enemy's position, noting movements of detachments of the enemy on the Emmetsburg Road, the relative positions for manœuvre, the lofty perch of the enemy, the rocky slopes from it, all making the position clearly defensive, I said, 'We could not call the enemy to a position better suited to our plans. All that we have to do is to file around his left and secure good ground between him and his capital.' I was not a little surprised at his impatience as, striking the air with his closed hand, he said, 'If he is there to-morrow I will attack him.' I answered, 'If he is there to-morrow it will be because he wants you to attack,' and queried, 'If that height has become the objective, why not take it at once? We have 40,000 men, less the casualties of the day; he cannot have more than 20,000.'"

In following the history of this great battle during the two following days it will be well for the reader to keep in mind the foregoing statement by Longstreet, of his conversation with Lee, and their points of difference, as they surveyed from Seminary Ridge the new position taken up by the Union army, and not later than half-past four o'clock of July first.

Lee was a man of genius, and in that respect may be called a great man. Great men are apt to make great mistakes. The pages of history are replete with illustrations of this fact. Napoleon, the greatest military genius, probably, that the world has ever produced, made mistakes that no ordinary man of sound common sense would have made; and the great Confederate commander was no exception to the rule. Honoured by the people of his State and of the Nation; educated at the expense of the Government; lifted into greatness by the Republic; he had drawn his sword against her in the hour of her peril, and had become her greatest adversary and most resourceful enemy. This was the great mistake of Lee's life.

Lee was a great general. His enemies in the Civil War all admitted that fact, and the world admits it to-day. He was the idol of his army, and the inspiration of the seceding States; but when he abandoned his defensive policy, wherein he chiefly excelled, and carried the war into the North, he made his great military mistake. As Shakespeare hath truly said, —

> " There is a tide in the affairs of men
> Which, taken at the flood, leads on to fortune."

Lee had made every preparation to ride the flood-tide of fortune. Behind the Rappahannock's protecting hills he had marshalled an army that was the pride of his ambitious heart, and the hope of the Rebellion. He was playing a bold game for a stupendous stake. His lieutenants were generals of marked ability, tested and tempered in the fiery ordeal of battle on many occasions. To him and to his cause they were known to be true as refined steel.

His officers of field and staff were brave and efficient, and every soldier in his mighty army was ready to bear every hardship of march, to dare every danger of battle, that their great chieftain thought necessary. No army in the world since the days of Alexander the Great was ever held more completely in the power of one directing hand. No leader of men or of armies, except Alexander, ever stood among his generals so supremely their leader and their Commander-in-Chief.

In every movement since assuming command of the Army of Northern Virginia in front of Richmond in 1862, he had handled his divisions with consummate skill. He had outgeneralled McClellan in front of Richmond, Pope, in front of Washington, Burnside in front of Fredericksburg, and Hooker at Chancellorsville. In this campaign he had outgeneralled Hooker and invaded Pennsylvania without a serious battle. So far, he had outgeneralled Meade and his corps commanders, by keeping his own army well in hand while he separated the Union commands widely, one from the other. He would meet and defeat the corps of the Union army in detail, and sweeping the last opposition from his path, swoop down upon our national capital, and dictate terms of peace to a nation humiliated and overthrown, thereby establishing the supremacy and independence of the Southern Confederacy. Such was the dream of success, such the assured hope of victory that swelled the proud heart of R. E. Lee, and inspired his warriors for battle, as he met our thin columns — a fourth of the Army of the Potomac — at Gettysburg.

Up to half-past four, or five o'clock P.M. of July first, Lee had everything his own way, except that the first detail from the Army of the Potomac had put up a fight that surprised him. The first of July, 1863, was Lee's high tide of victory (his tide of defeat came later), for the Union army had been driven from its first position in confusion, and fully expected to be attacked in its second position. But Lee established his headquarters at a small brick house fronting the Chambersburg Pike, just over the crest of Seminary Ridge to the westward, and for the time being seemed perfectly satisfied with what his army had accomplished. If Lee intended to continue the Battle of Gettysburg, then this was his great mistake of the campaign; and certainly between his failure to continue the battle that night and his attack and battle on our chosen position the next day, occurred the mistake that eliminated from his grasp the last reasonable hope of victory. Assuming that Lee intended to do exactly what, at half-past four o'clock on July first he said to Longstreet he would do, namely, "If he is there to-morrow I will attack him," then why he did not follow up with his wonted vigour the advantage already gained is beyond the comprehension of every one familiar with the conditions.

General Gordon, speaking of our retreat on the first of July, says: "In less than one-half hour my troops would have swept up and over those hills, the possession of which was of such momentous consequence. It is not surprising, with the full realization of the consequences of a halt, that I should have refused at first to obey the order. Not until the third or fourth order of the most peremptory character reached me, did I obey." Very likely, if Gordon had not been ordered to halt, he would have realized that he had been in a fight before his "troops swept up and over those hills"; but surely that was the time to try.

It may be said that Lee's army was weary with its long march, and with the battle that had been so stubbornly contested; but what was the comparative condition of Howard's and Doubleday's forces on the opposing line at the same hour?

Longstreet, in his reply to Lee, above quoted, urging the renewal of the battle at once, said: "We have 40,000 men, less the casualties of the day; he cannot have more than 20,000." In this off-hand estimate of strength Longstreet was not far from correct. To Hill's and Ewell's battle strength of seventeen brigades, had been added Anderson's division of Hill's corps, comprising five additional brigades, swelling Lee's entire strength on the ground to twenty-two brigades, or about 44,000. What the Confederate losses were during the day, we have no means of knowing, only one of their division commanders having made a report; but General Heth, whose division opened the battle with Buford, and was later met by Wadsworth's division of the First Corps, says, in his report: "In less than twenty-five minutes my division lost 2,700 men in killed and wounded." Heth also lost a thousand prisoners, on the authority of Longstreet, swelling Heth's entire loss to 3,700. If the losses sustained by Pender's and Rodes' divisions were nearly equal to Heth's — and we have every reason to believe they were — to say nothing of Early's loss, which was small, the total Confederate loss must have been fully 9,000, which would leave 35,000 men in line, ready to renew the battle at five o'clock P.M. of July first, if Lee had given the word.

On the other hand, in the battle just ended, the Union commanders had lost nearly half of their number. Buford's division had lost 500, the First Corps 5,500, the Eleventh Corps 2,500, or an aggregate of 8,500; and, after suffering the discouragement of defeat, they awaited the renewal of the onset by their victorious opponents, while they prayed God, as soldiers pray, that Lee would do exactly what he did — give us a rest until Meade arrived with the other portion of the Union army.

GETTYSBURG

In line on Cemetery Hill the Union forces comprised Buford's cavalry division, 2,500 strong, the First Corps 3,000, and the Eleventh Corps 7,200, the remnants of the divisions that had borne the brunt of the battle; in all, 12,700 men. To those may be added Slocum's Twelfth Corps, which arrived on the ground about the time our broken columns reached Cemetery Hill; for General Slocum made the best time of all in coming to our rescue.

Slocum's corps numbered 8,500, and extended our line to the left along Cemetery Ridge; but later, and during the night, it took a position on our right from the crest of Culp's Hill to Rock Creek. With this reinforcement of the Twelfth Corps, Howard commanded a force of 21,200 men, at five o'clock P.M., to meet Lee's expected attack with 35,000, and there was not another Union regiment within eight hours' march of his position. What was even worse, Meade had not yet ordered the concentration of the remaining four infantry corps and two cavalry divisions of his army at Gettysburg, and they were quietly and peacefully resting from ten to twenty-two miles away; but Lee, from his exalted viewpoint on Seminary Ridge, looking across the wide intervening valley to the Union lines in hurrying formation on Cemetery Hill, only said, as he struck the air with his clinched hand, "If he is there to-morrow I will attack him."

Whatever Lee's reasons may have been for not attacking that night, they were perfectly satisfactory to that weary portion of the Union army, hard at work intrenching their position on Cemetery Hill; and equally satisfactory to the whole army was his conclusion to attack that strong position, so easily avoided, on the following day, provided he would delay that attack until General Meade could and would concentrate his army; but why a general of Lee's genius and daring should have continued the battle then or ever, in such a disadvantageous position for him, especially after General Meade had partially concentrated his army there and chosen his battle-ground, passes all understanding.

Before starting out on his invasion of the North, Lee had agreed with his corps commanders to make his campaign one of defensive tactics; which means, simply, avoiding the giving of battle in the enemy's chosen position, and compelling the enemy, if possible, to attack him in his chosen, defensive position. Lee had perfect confidence in the fighting strength of his army, and in the military skill and ability of his generals; while that army, to a man, had supreme confidence in their leaders, and especially in their commander-in-chief. Longstreet, speaking of his own corps, says: "The First Corps was as a solid rock, a great rock. It was not to be broken of good position by direct assault, and was steady enough to work and wait for its chosen battle." And of Lee's army, as a whole, Longstreet adds, after enumerating the comparative appointments and advantages of the opposing armies: "We were prepared to march cheerfully forward and accept the gauge, hoping by strategic skill to throw the onus of battle upon the enemy."

General Gordon also speaks of Lee's army before joining battle on the first of July, as of "compact ranks, boundless confidence, and exultant hopes, as proud and puissant an army as was ever marshalled." Nor were Lee's generals lacking in

confidence in their own ability as leaders in the field;
and Lee himself so confidently believed in his own
superior generalship, that he seemed frequently to
ignore the very existence of the Union generals
who were opposed to him.

Therefore, from every military standpoint,
illumed by all the sidelights of human experience
that could be brought to bear on the situation, Lee
should have won the Battle of Gettysburg; and
almost every event of march and manœuvre and
battle, up to the closing hours of July first, was
most decidedly favourable to him and to his cause.
But it was written among the eternal stars that the
final result should be otherwise.

When Lee crossed the South Mountain Range
and came face to face with his old antagonist, the
Army of the Potomac, we find him unaccountably
nervous, impatient, hesitating. "If he is there
to-morrow, I will attack him," tells the story. That
one sentence expresses more than many pages.
Why should he attack a strong defensive position
at any time, when it was so plainly in his power to
flank and avoid it? It was necessary to fight the

battle of July first, for Buford and Reynolds and Howard were in his path; but that battle was won, and his pathway clear. The Union army had been driven to Cemetery Hill — to a strong defensive position but most unfavourable for offensive operations against Lee's further movements, and for that night at least, absolutely out of his way; for a beautiful undulating valley more than a mile wide, stretching away to the southward, lay between him and his helpless enemy. Why should he turn aside, and go out of his way to buck against a fighting foeman's stronghold, when he could rest his army in peace from five o'clock until midnight, and then have plenty of time to slip quietly along the west side of the wide valley, with Seminary Ridge at his back, and no enemy near enough to detect or disturb his march? In two hours he could have been south of Howard's rock-ribbed citadels, cutting Meade's army in two without a battle, and compelling that portion on Cemetery Hill and Ridge to abandon its worthless position and hurry southward to join, if possible, the other wing in saving their communications and covering the national capital. He did not do it, however, and for once, at least, Lee's courage failed him. It must be conceded that, as a man and a general, he was not usually lacking in physical courage; but in that respect he was no braver than the rank and file of his army. Here, however, we find him lacking in that physical courage so necessary in the commander of an army. Here was a brilliant chance of war, greatly in his favour, that Lee dared not take. Behind his position on Seminary Ridge ran the Hagerstown Road in a southwestward direction through the South Mountain Range to the crossings of the Potomac, and Lee, with all his genius, and all his warlike daring, refused to abandon that back-door for a safe retreat to the Potomac and Virginia, in the event that he should meet with defeat.

General R. H. Anderson, commanding the first division of Hill's corps, reported a conversation with General Lee at about twelve o'clock noon of July first, in which Lee said: "I am in ignorance as to what we have in front of us here. It may be the whole Federal army, or it may be only a detach-

PRESIDENT JEFFERSON DAVIS

GENERAL ROBERT E. LEE

ment. If it is the whole Federal force, we must fight a battle here. If we do not gain a victory, those defiles and gorges which we passed this morning will shelter us from disaster."

So it would seem that Lee had lost much of his confidence, and was looking for disaster, and a sheltered retreat. For that reason he clung to the Hagerstown Road, and used it for that purpose.

CHAPTER XII

G ENERAL JOHN F. REYNOLDS was graduated from West Point in 1841. He was thereafter commissioned a lieutenant of artillery, and in the Mexican War he won the brevets of Captain at Monterey and of Major at Buena Vista. When the Civil War broke out in 1861, he was commissioned a Brigadier-General, and commanded a brigade in McClellan's peninsula campaign, and a division under Pope at the second Bull Run, in 1862. In November of that year he was appointed a Major-General, and placed in command of the First Corps of the Army of the Potomac, which position he held in the Fredericksburg and Chancellorsville campaigns, and during the toilsome march to Pennsylvania in June. He was in command of the right wing of our army, comprising the First, Third, and Eleventh Corps, and Buford's cavalry division, at the time of his death, on July first, at Gettysburg.

General Reynolds was a man of more than ordinary ability on the march and in the field. His corps, to a man, looked upon him as a reliable soldier, patriotic, and devoted to the Union cause, but above and beyond all else a general devoted to the care of the soldiers under his command, and true to their rights as American citizens, engaged with himself in the common cause of nationality.

In our experience of four years in the army, as a Union soldier, we frequently had occasion to notice that, while the five senses seemed as well developed among that class known in the army as generals, as among the larger class known as common soldiers, that most important of all the senses — the sixth, or common sense — was not so well developed in them. Common sense may be defined as good sense; that is to say, a man who is sensible and of good judgment in common, everyday affairs possesses common sense. We call that man sensible whose acts and conduct in matters of practical concern are marked and governed by sound judgment.

Taking the foregoing as a true and correct defini-
tion of the term, one is surprised at the dearth of
generals in our army during the Civil War (and
probably in all other armies of all other wars) who
possessed a fair quantity and fair quality of
common sense.

A general above all men, should have the good
sense to know that the soldiers of his command are
human beings, subject to human ailments, and need
and deserve all the care that he can possibly give
them in everything pertaining to the daily routine
of life in camp and on the march, in order that they
may, when the hour of battle comes, arrive on the
firing line in condition to give the best possible
service to their cause. But alas, how few of them
seem to consider these simple but important matters
worthy of their genius! We have more than once
seen and experienced, after a wearisome day's
march, on going into camp at night, and after the
fires were kindled and the soldiers were engaged in
preparing their supper, a whole corps of troops
moved by their commander, from one to three
hundred yards, where they were obliged to relight

their camp-fires before they could procure their supper and take the rest that they so greatly needed, and all on account of the lack of just a little common sense in their general.

We have marched and countermarched for a full hour, when the shades of night were falling, after marching all day in the rain and mud, following our general and his staff while they rode their horses hither and thither as they hunted up convenient headquarters for the general to pass the night under a roof.

How the soldiers would curse on such occasions! Not that they objected to the general finding a convenient, or even luxurious resting-place for himself and staff, if only he would apply the rules of common sense to our condition, which he failed to do.

But to cap the climax. On a hot July day, when the old veteran held the position of captain in a certain brigade, the following event occurred not far from Petersburg, Va. We were returning to rejoin our corps from the right of our lines, where our whole brigade had been engaged for a week in building fortifications; but, regardless of our com-

fort, the general rode with his staff on a full gallop
from the rear to the front, through the whole length
of the brigade, keeping the centre of the road and
scattering his regiments to the right and to the left,
and for no reason under the sun except that he had
no common sense, and wanted to show his authority
and high-mightiness. Oh, how the soldiers of that
brigade did respect and honour their general from
that day, and forever after ! If it had been necessary for the general and his staff to ride to the
front, how easily an officer could have ridden a little
in advance and directed each regiment to oblique
to the right or left, as he might designate, and thus
give the general free passage without in any manner disturbing the orderly formation and march of
the brigade for a single moment. In the presence
of an enemy the act would have been murderous,
and could have been done only by a fool or a mad-
man. With no enemy within miles of us, as was
the case, the act was the most brazen display of
big-headed pomposity that we ever witnessed. But
we are glad to be able to report that such acts

were infrequent in our army, and we never saw it repeated.

We have joined in many a march in old Virginia, when the days were long and hot, and the power of the soldiers to endure the fatigue of the march and keep their places in the ranks was greatly enhanced by an opportunity to brew a cup of coffee by the wayside from time to time. This fact was well known by every general in the Army of the Potomac, and the practice was never forbidden by any of them, so far as we can remember; but at the same time we were generally obliged to take our chances during our moments of rest that were occasionally ordered, in building fires for that purpose, not knowing the length of time the rest would continue. We were obliged to guess at it, and by guess many a camp-fire was built in vain, and many a half-steeped cup of coffee thrown into the dust; for our generals were men of genius, contemplating, as they rode on the march, the shock of armies in battle, and the mighty deeds they would accomplish when they aligned for action these very soldiers. They knew that the men were tried and true, yet they considered them so far beneath their notice on the march that they entirely overlooked, for their convenience, this simple matter of coffee-making. The reader can readily imagine the inconvenience, and the loss of coffee and rest — to both of which we were entitled — by the lack of common sense on the part of our generals. He can imagine also how the soldiers would curse, until the very atmosphere was blue, and brimstone seemed to smoke on the hot stones of the highway, when, after wasting the time that should have been devoted to needed rest, in getting their fires all ablaze and their coffee-pails in place, with the water close to the boiling point, the notes of the bugle announced that the march would forthwith be resumed.

We mention these little circumstances of bygone days — hundreds of which we have seen and experienced — in order to compare with them the common-sense methods practised by General Reynolds toward his corps while on the march. He was the only corps commander under whom we had the honour of serving during the Civil War (and we served under several) whose acts of common sense are a pleasure to remember. There was another general in the Army of the Potomac in whose brigade we were numbered, who watched and provided with the same care and consideration over his brigade, that General Reynolds exercised toward his corps, and that commander was General Gibbon. We did not serve under Gibbon after he took command of a division, but we have reason to believe that General Gibbon never lost his common sense.

During our first campaigns under the command of General Reynolds, in the Fall and Winter of 1862, our marches were not long, and the weather was not extremely hot until after the Chancellorsville campaign was ended, in May, but even then we had learned to look upon him as a sensible man in every respect, and a reliable general in the field and on the march. It was not, however, until the Gettysburg campaign opened, that we learned the true value of such a commander. The First Corps broke camp on the north side of the Rappahannock River, opposite Fredericksburg, on the morning of the twelfth day of June, and started on that wearisome march of about one hundred and sixty miles, which terminated at Gettysburg on July first. Some days our marches were short, and some days we rested in camp and did not march at all; but on other occasions, like unto the long hot June days of Virginia, we made long, hot, and tedious marches. It was particularly on those trying occasions that we learned to appreciate the superior ability of General Reynolds in caring for his troops and providing for their comfort, by a little timely forethought, the best and not the worst that could be obtained for them in the field.

Whether the march of the day was long or short, whenever a halt was made for a sufficient length of time, a staff officer carried the General's order to every regiment in the corps, "You will have time to make coffee if you so desire." If we did not receive that order no man started a fire, and during the whole march there was never a fire lighted in vain. What a relief it was to the thousands of men who wore the First Corps badge, to know for a certainty that they could rest in peace, if the halt was intended for a rest only; and if the halt was to be long enough to make coffee, we would be so informed. Then, when we halted for the night and went into camp at the end of the day's march, there was no moving of weary regiments from one point to another; for the position for the encampment was selected in advance by the General himself, or by a staff officer, and each brigade commander, as he came up with his command, was directed where to place his brigade, and where he would find water and wood for his regiments. There was no confusion, no waste of time. It was all very simple, but it did require considerable extra care and trouble on the part of the corps commander; and we soldiers of the First Corps were very thankful that our General had, not only common sense, but sufficient humanity in his heart to use it. After we crossed the Potomac into Maryland, on the twenty-fifth of June, there was a change in the weather, and it rained every day or night, and some of the time both day and night, until the first of July; but the General's care for his troops never slackened.

On that campaign the boys of the First Corps applied to General Reynolds the sobriquet of "Old Common Sense," in their appreciation of his remarkable supply of that commodity; yet he was not old in years, only forty-three when he was killed, but old in comparison to the rank and file of his corps, who were only boys of from sixteen to twenty-five; and especially was he old in practical wisdom to care for the everyday needs of his soldiers, as compared with other generals in command of army corps.

To double-quick in the heat of the day from one part of a battlefield to another, in order to meet the enemy in some unexpected quarter; to move hastily to a stronger or more desirable position when in proximity with or in the presence of the enemy; to move half the army, or the whole of it for that matter; to change the positions of brigades, divisions, and corps, in order to make an encampment more secure from attack—all these are incidents in a soldier's life and duty that he accepts cheerfully, no matter what the inconvenience or hardship imposed thereby; but to be hack-hammered from pillar to post, when weary, footsore, and hungry, just to satisfy the senseless whim of a general running over with selfish egotism, is, to say the least, trying on a soldier's nerves.

On the morning of July first, 1863, when General Reynolds found himself on the soil of his native State, with Lee's whole army in his front, the question may arise, Did he act wisely and with that discretion which is the better part of valour? From all the surrounding conditions at the time it would seem that he made a great mistake in opening the battle. General Meade's headquarters were at Taneytown, fifteen miles to the southward, and his army was widely scattered and out of touch for at least the next twelve hours with Reynolds' command. Meade's orders to Reynolds seem to have been to uncover Lee's army and fall back to Pipe Creek, delaying Lee's march as much as possible, while notifying Meade so that he might concentrate his army for a general and decisive battle. However, when Reynolds uncovered Lee's army he sent a despatch to Meade to the effect that the heights of Gettysburg was the place to fight the battle, and that he would hold the position with the right wing while Meade concentrated his army at that point. Then Reynolds plunged the First Corps into battle to support Buford's cavalry division, and called the Eleventh and Third Corps to his assistance, the latter of which did not reach the field that day, and the very life of the troops engaged was fought out long before reinforcements arrived. As Reynolds was killed in the very beginning of the battle, it is impossible to say what his intentions may have been, but it is certain that there was no concert of action between the generals, and this lack of harmony must have led to disaster, but for the fact that Reynolds' mistake was followed by a greater mistake on the part of Lee. As Reynolds rode up from the southward on the morning of July first, through the whole length of the wide valley stretching between Seminary Ridge on the west and Cemetery Hill and Ridge on the east, he must have assumed that Lee's whole army was west of Seminary Ridge and that he could maintain his position thereon until the whole of Meade's army arrived. After Reynolds' death, when Ewell's corps came in upon us from the northeast, taking Howard's right in reverse, there was nothing left for Howard to do but seek refuge on Cemetery Hill. If Reynolds knew of the situation of Ewell's corps within the Susquehanna Valley, he must have relied on finally retreating to Cemetery Hill, just as Howard did, and that Lee would continue the battle there. As Lee did that very thing, it may be assumed that Reynolds' battle of July first was not a mistake but a strategic movement that resulted in final victory, although General Reynolds lost his life in carrying it to success.

Four years of service in the army did not incline the old veteran toward hero-worship, but after nearly half a century he still remembers that toilsome march from Fredericksburg to Gettysburg in 1863, as among the pleasant recollections of those strenuous war days; and while life remains he will remember that dark, silent, alert man who commanded the First Corps, with a feeling of profound veneration. General John F. Reynolds may not be represented in Statuary Hall of the national capitol, beside the Father and Preserver of the country, but his statue stands in the wide Hall of Fame on Cemetery Hill, within the great battle-field where he gave his life in the cause for which the immortal Lincoln died; and there shall it stand for all time, truthfully representing a patriot and common-sense general.

CHAPTER XIII

MEADE'S STRATEGY

GENERAL REYNOLDS' despatch, sent about nine o'clock on the morning of July first, stating that he had met Lee's army, and that the heights of Gettysburg was the place for the battle, reached General Meade at Taneytown just as soon as a good horse could carry it to him, probably by eleven o'clock. But General Meade did not order his army to concentrate at Gettysburg. He was preparing to meet Lee at Pipe Creek, whom he expected to follow Reynolds' retiring column, and to attack him in his chosen position. Lee had started out on an offensive campaign, and it was Meade's intention that he should continue the offensive, and give battle in some strong position that Meade hoped to select. For that purpose Meade had established his headquarters at Taneytown, and selected a defensive position at Pipe Creek, in what appeared to be, and in fact was, a suitable position for the mobilization of his army, when he should discover Lee and succeed in calling him in that direction. While Meade's army was widely scattered, it was in a far better condition for concentration at Pipe Creek than at Gettysburg. General Hunt, with the artillery reserve, was with him at Taneytown, and the Second Corps under the command of Hancock was not far away, while the Fifth Corps was at Union Mills, the Sixth Corps at Manchester, and the Third Corps, which was part of the right wing, was still as near Taneytown as Gettysburg.

Meade, it must be confessed, was not a great general. He had been in command of the Army of the Potomac less than four days; in fact he was then only nominally in command. He did not know his army, and outside of the Fifth Corps that he had previously commanded, the army knew but very little about Meade. Each corps commander seemed to have a general idea of the situation and of his duties, and tried to do the best he could according to the light he possessed, but to the army the situation was far from encouraging. The results of Fredericksburg and Chancellorsville had not inspired us with confidence in our generals, and the great lack of harmony among them at that time was sufficient to fill all hearts with foreboding.

The Army of the Potomac was a splendid body of men, with confidence in its ability to defeat Lee, if once put into position to meet him squarely in battle. The danger was that Lee, by superior generalship, would defeat us in detail, one or two corps at a time. With the Army of the Potomac united, it mattered little to us who our general might be, but the all-important question was, Would Meade display sufficient generalship to unite his army? General Meade lacked confidence in his own ability as a general. In plain English, he was afraid of Lee. Very likely he had good and sufficient reasons to fear Lee's generalship. Probably every prominent general in the Army of the Potomac, except perhaps General Hooker (and in that Hooker was clearly wrong), considered Lee superior as a general to Meade, or to himself; but that fact did not deter Reynolds from doing his best to put up a winning battle against him on the first of July. It did not deter Howard from taking up the battle where Reynolds laid it down with his life, and making every effort toward a soldierly disposition of his small force to hold Cemetery Hill as long as good fighting could hold it. It did not deter Slocum from marching his corps to the assistance of those already on the battlefield, without orders from the commanding general, but from the fact that he had learned that the battle was on, and that his corps was needed on the firing line.

Still it must have been a severe disappointment to General Meade when he learned that Reynolds had opened the battle at Gettysburg, for it was good strategy on Meade's part to concentrate his army in a defensive position before the battle was opened, or at least to have his army well in hand, so that it should not be destroyed piecemeal. General Meade, through the aid of his engineers, had selected a strong defensive line behind Pipe Creek, in a position approved by General Halleck, the Commander-in-Chief at Washington, as well as by himself, covering both Washington and Baltimore by lines that could not be turned. How could it be expected that he would abandon this carefully selected position, with his strongest corps near at hand and convenient for the concentration of his whole army, and rush pell-mell to Gettysburg to support the battle in that vicinity? Meade could not, in justice to himself and his position, act with undue haste, and he called to his aid in counsel at that trying hour, no less a person than General Hancock, commander of the Second Corps. The outcome of that consultation was that Meade directed Hancock to ride to Gettysburg, view the situation there, and report the condition as he found it. More than that, Meade delegated to Hancock the authority of Commander-in-Chief for the time being, leaving it within his discretion whether or not to retreat from Gettysburg to Pipe Creek, or order the army to concentrate at Gettysburg. General Meade reserved for himself no choice in the matter. He left the entire situation to Hancock's judgment, hoping, no doubt, that he would decide against Gettysburg for the battle-ground; but when he decided in its favour Meade was compelled to reinforce that point with his whole army.

GETTYSBURG

General Hancock arrived on Cemetery Hill about half-past four o'clock, just as Howard's broken lines were there gathered in confusion. We are informed by General Doubleday in his account of Gettysburg, that he was present on Cemetery Hill when Hancock rode up to Howard and informed him that, by the direction of General Meade, he would assume command of the field. To this General Howard objected, replying: "No, General, you cannot take command here, as I am your senior in rank." Then Hancock said he would return and report to General Meade in person. To this General Howard also objected, saying: "That will not do either, as I need you here to assist in forming these lines." Hancock was a superb man, ready to obey as well as command. General Grant afterwards said of him: "Hancock stands the most conspicuous figure of all our general officers who did not exercise a separate command." So Hancock remained with Howard and gave him all the assistance in his power. Strange to say, however, after viewing the lay of the country — the strong position — the wide valley in front and Seminary Ridge beyond, occupied by the Confederates in force, with an unobstructed gateway for a movement by their right flank to the southward that would entirely uncover our position, Hancock approved of the Gettysburg hills as the field whereon to continue the battle, and sent a despatch to General Meade to that effect.

When General Meade received Hancock's despatch, about eight o'clock in the evening, Hancock was at Gettysburg actively making preparations for the battle of the coming day, provided Lee would attack and not slip away from our front. So Meade gave up his carefully selected position, and issued the order for every absent division to advance on Gettysburg, with all possible haste.

General Meade and staff reached Cemetery Hill about midnight, where he established his headquarters in a little old one-story frame house or shack on the west side of the Taneytown Road, three hundred yards east of the crest of the southern prolongation of Cemetery Hill, and about four hundred yards south of the west gate of the Cemetery. The same old shack stood there in 1900.

GETTYSBURG

After the arrival of General Meade on Cemetery Hill a council of war was held by the Union generals then present, and Meade, not being satisfied with the conditions presented to him, gave it as his opinion that Gettysburg was not the place to fight a battle. His generals, however, without a dissenting voice (General Sickles had not yet arrived) favoured no retreat from the position they then held, to Pipe Creek or any other place, without a fight. There certainly was no objection to a battle in that strong position, provided that Lee was willing to attack; but if he slipped past us, what then? That was exactly what Meade feared. General Halleck, in a despatch from Washington, expressed the fear that his position was too far to the eastward; to which Meade replied, during the forenoon, that in the event he should find the Confederates moving to interpose between his army and Washington, he would fall back on his supplies at Westminster.

During the night of July first, the soldiers in battle-line of both armies rested on their arms, while their absent comrades, under urgent orders to reach the field, rested on their feet. There is no other ordeal so severe and trying to a soldier as a night-march, but this was an occasion for the greatest of human efforts, and throughout the silent hours of that July night they plodded on.

Before the morning of July second dawned, Lee's whole army, with the exception of Pickett's division and Stuart's cavalry, had arrived on the field, and it might be presumed that he was ready for battle. His left rested on Rock Creek, east of Gettysburg, and comprised Ewell's corps; Johnson's division near Culp's Hill; Early's and Rodes' divisions, extending the Confederate line to the right through the city; Pender's division of the Third Corps on the right of Rodes, with the other divisions of the Third Corps resting on Seminary Ridge around and near general headquarters.

Lee's centre was commanded by A. P. Hill. His right was commanded by Longstreet, whose troops were the last to arrive on the field, and for some unaccountable reason seemed a long time in getting into position.

When the morning of July second dawned, the condition of Meade's army had greatly improved.

Not only had the troops in line at sunset rested and recuperated their strength and courage, but Hancock's Second Corps, 13,000 strong, had arrived on the field, and extended Howard's former line to the left, southward along Cemetery Ridge toward Round Top.

The Second Corps came upon the field over the Taneytown Road, from three to four hundred yards in rear of the ridge upon which Hancock, with Meade's approval, had selected his position, so that as each division arrived opposite its place in line, it moved forward to the point selected on the ridge, and the weary soldiers dropped to repose, but ready for battle at any moment when the signal sounded. The Second Corps made our line of battle about 34,000 strong, extending from Rock Creek on the right, in a northwesterly direction along the slope of Culp's Hill to its crest; thence westward to the west gate of the Cemetery on the Taneytown Road, and thence southward along the crest of Cemetery Ridge half way to Round Top. The Twelfth Corps held the right of our line extending to the crest of Culp's Hill, the north front of which was held by Wadsworth's division of the First Corps, on Slocum's left. To the left of Wadsworth, across the valley between Culp's Hill and Cemetery Hill, and along the north and northwest fronts of Cemetery Hill were stationed the three divisions of the Eleventh Corps. To the left of the Eleventh Corps, facing the west front of Cemetery Hill, were the second and third divisions of the First Corps. To the left and south of Doubleday's two divisions the Second Corps extended our line southward along Cemetery Ridge for the full length of Hancock's three divisions, and Buford's cavalry division — which is here counted in the aggregate of Meade's 34,000 — acted as a reserve force for the protection of our flanks and the reinforcement of any point suddenly put in jeopardy.

The Third Corps, commanded by General Sickles, 12,000 strong, also arrived on the field at an early hour in the morning. This gave Meade a force of 46,000 men all told, to meet Lee's army, very early on the morning of July second. Thus it appears that General Meade had employed the night to great advantage, and had made every effort in his power to unite his army so that he might in his first battle meet his great antagonist on somewhere near equal terms. Still the Fifth Corps, commanded by General Sykes, 12,500 strong, and the Sixth Corps, commanded by General Sedgwick, 15,500 strong (28,000 in all, or more than one-third of Meade's whole army), were many weary miles away. Would Lee take advantage of the fact that a third of Meade's army was still absent? If he intended, or desired, to pursue his tactics of previous battles, and defeat his opponents in detail, here indeed was his opportunity. But Lee had lost his balance, and there followed the continuation of his hesitating policy of the afternoon before. Hour after hour passed, with only an occasional picket shot, or the solitary boom of a heavy gun, and every hour's delay added to Meade's advantage. Probably there never was a time in the history of the Army of the Potomac, when it stood in greater need of a direct interposition of the hand of God in its behalf, especially at five o'clock in the afternoon of July first, and Lee's inaction at that time and during the greater part of the next day (a weakness so foreign to his character on all previous occasions) seems to have been in response to that trying need. He wavered; he hesitated; he waited, — while our army concentrated. From five o'clock P.M. of July first to four o'clock P.M. of July second, Lee was apparently asleep; and by that twenty-three hours of inaction his flood tide of fortune had ebbed, and the wild dream of his ambition had passed beyond all chance of fulfilment.

CHAPTER XIV

LINES WHICH WERE AND LINES WHICH WERE NOT FORMED

BETWEEN the southern prolongation of Cemetery Hill, which terminates in Round Top two and a half miles to the southward, and the Seminary Ridge opposite, there lies a beautiful, irregular valley, about two and one-half miles in length, by from a mile to a mile and a quarter in width. This valley is divided into two irregular triangles by the Emmetsburg Road, which follows a well-defined ridge across and from the western slope of Cemetery Hill, in a southwesterly direction, until the ridge merges into and the road crosses Seminary Ridge, about a mile almost due west from Round Top. The eastern triangle has its apex toward the north, its base extending from Seminary Ridge to Round Top and its perpendicular extending northward along the easternmost of these three ridges, from Round Top to Cemetery Hill. The western triangle is the reverse of the eastern, its base extending from Cemetery Hill about a mile and an eighth west to Seminary Ridge, its perpendicular running southward along the ridge for the distance of two and one-half miles, the juncture of the Seminary with the Emmetsburg Road Ridge forming its apex. The Emmetsburg Road, therefore, forms the hypothenuse of both the aforesaid triangles.

This valley, which may truly be called the Valley of Gettysburg, continues past the base of Cemetery Hill and the city far away to the northward; while to the southward beyond Round Top it spreads out in limitless extent.

The eastern of the afore-mentioned ridges, occupied by Hancock's corps from Cemetery Hill half way to Little Round Top, is the least prominent of the three. In fact, for more than half the distance, and throughout the whole right wing of Hancock's line, the ridge is nothing more than a gentle elevation. The Emmetsburg Road Ridge is more prominent, and west of Hancock's left, and the unoccupied space between his left and Little

Round Top, shuts off the view of the Seminary Ridge beyond. The Seminary Ridge is the most commanding ridge of the three, and from the point opposite Hancock's centre southward to its juncture with the Emmetsburg Road, it becomes abrupt, rocky, and heavily wooded.

General Sickles, in command of the Third Corps, marched to Gettysburg in the early morning of July second, along the Emmetsburg Road. At the time he crossed the Seminary Ridge, two and one-half miles southwest of Cemetery Hill, Longstreet, with his Confederates, was resting among the groves and on the grassy slopes of the same ridge farther to the northward and from a mile and a half to two miles west of Hancock's right.

Sickles noticed the splendid formation of the Emmetsburg Road Ridge, both for defensive and offensive operations, with a broad highway running along its whole length to facilitate the movement of troops, and especially artillery, from one point to another in the line, and very naturally desired to avail himself of such a strategic position. General Sickles noticed something more. In this wide-open valley he saw a most inviting gateway for Lee to do exactly what Longstreet had been urging him to do—slip quietly past Meade's defensive position on Cemetery Hill and Ridge, under the cover of night, or under the cover of Seminary Ridge if he cared to make such a movement in broad day, and align his army between the Army of the Potomac and Washington, thereby compelling Meade to give battle upon ground of Lee's own choosing. This same view of the situation had caused Meade to express the opinion that Gettysburg was not the place to fight the battle. However, General Meade seemed to think that Cemetery Ridge was a stronger and more secure position, and he instructed Sickles to form his corps on Hancock's left, extending his line southward to Little Round Top. At least, General Meade so claimed afterwards, but probably, not caring to assume the whole responsibility, he gave such orders as Sickles construed into discretionary authority in selecting his position, and Sickles selected the line of the Emmetsburg Road. This blunder, or want of understanding between the generals, threw our battle formation out of all harmony, and may, or may not, have worked to the disadvantage of the Union cause the second day.

General Meade was extremely cautious, too cautious to be apt to win a great victory like the capture or annihilation of the army opposed to him, and in this instance he had every reason to be cautious from the fact that a third of his army was still far away from the field. Meade reasoned that as Lee had marched his army far from his base, and had actually carried the war into a locality unknown to him, it would be the proper thing to encourage him to fight a truly offensive battle on grounds of Meade's own choosing; and certainly he did not wish to assume a position, if he could possibly avoid it, that would occasion the renewal of the contest before the arrival of the Fifth and Sixth Corps. The longer Lee delayed his attack, assuming that he would certainly attack Meade's chosen position, the more advantageous the situation became.

By extending Hancock's line southward along Cemetery Ridge to Round Top, Meade would have a strong, compact position, with his left absolutely secure. The Fifth Corps was approaching the field by the Taneytown Road, and would arrive in the exact locality to reinforce readily any part of his west front, as the Taneytown Road runs the whole length of Cemetery Ridge and only three or four hundred yards in rear of the crest. Sickles' corps, nearly 12,000 strong, was ample to form an invincible battle-line from Hancock's left to that impregnable bastion to the southward.

Because of the absence of the Fifth and Sixth Corps, but for no other reason, was Meade justified in placing his army in such a purely defensive position; for, to abandon the Emmetsburg Road to Longstreet was in itself a victory for Lee. The Emmetsburg and Hagerstown Roads both lead to the Potomac, and with these roads in his possession, Lee could readily retreat in absolute safety, in case of defeat.

There was another reason why the Emmetsburg Road should not have been given over to the possession of Longstreet at that time. It would have afforded a wide and unobstructed gateway for Lee's whole army to move by his right flank completely beyond and away from Meade's strong position, compelling Meade to evacuate, and retreat in haste, in order to interpose between Lee's army and Washington. Meade himself was fearful of that very movement; otherwise, being the commanding general, he would have said to Sickles in plain English, so there could have been no misunderstanding, "Form your corps on Hancock's left, and continue his line southward along the ridge to Little Round Top," and surely Sickles would have followed such instructions; but Meade simply did not care to assume the whole responsibility, so he gave a kind of ambiguous order that Sickles construed according to his ideas of the necessity of the case.

Sickles was a man of action, a born fighter; and his idea of holding a position that might readily be turned into the offensive, and especially of blocking Lee's open gateway to the flank and rear of Meade's position, was the correct one; provided, of course, that the army was strong enough and in a condition to assume it. Every soldier must admire Sickles' courage, and admit that he had weighty reasons for making the attempt to bring Lee to battle then and there, rather than take any chances on a flank movement and a battle later, in a less favourable position.

The distance from Cemetery Hill along the Emmetsburg Road Ridge to Seminary Ridge is only a trifle, if any, farther than from the same point southward along Cemetery Ridge to Round Top. Clearly the Emmetsburg Road Ridge was the line that should have been selected for our battle-line had Meade's whole army been on the field and ready to assume the position on the morning of July second. To assume such position would have necessitated the moving of Hancock's corps forward or westward to the Emmetsburg Road; which movement would have swung his left toward the front a half or three-fourths of a mile, while his right would still have been pivoted on the west gate of the Cemetery, thus giving Hancock a battle-line about a mile or a mile and a half in length, or the same length of the inner line as held by him, with his left far down the Emmetsburg Road about four or five hundred yards northeast of the point where it is crossed by the Wheatfield Road. Such formation would have carried Sickles' right half a mile farther southwest on the Emmetsburg Road than the point where he placed it; from which his battle-line would have followed the Emmetsburg Road to the Seminary Ridge, a mile or more farther toward the southwest.

Then with the Fifth Corps, had it been on the ground, to hold the left on Seminary Ridge, and the Sixth Corps in reserve, Meade could have fought Lee to a finish at any point and every point along his line, and followed up his success by sweeping northward with his reserve along the crest of Seminary Ridge, until, gaining possession of the Hagerstown Road, he would have cut off Lee's retreat and turned his defeat into rout and destruction.

But the Fifth and Sixth Corps were not there, and the preparation for battle was obliged to go on without them. Therefore, in the absence of 28,000 infantry and artillery, and until they should arrive, it may have been good generalship on Meade's part

to assume the strongest defensive position possible
and manœuvre to delay rather than to facilitate and
invite attack. Meade's idea was to watch the
enemy, and retreat hastily if he started to move
away from his front. Sickles' idea was to shove his
lines into the enemy's teeth.

The misunderstanding on the part of the generals was unaccountable. At the very time when
harmony in council and unity in action were necessary to insure success, harmony and unity were lacking. Neither position was selected. Hancock's line
was not extended to Little Round Top; Sickles'
line was not continued to Seminary Ridge. These
were the lines that were not formed. The lines
that were formed were, Hancock's in his old position along the crest of Cemetery Ridge; Sickles'
line away to the front, shooting out well toward
Seminary Ridge but not reaching it. Sickles
formed his corps in accordance with his own military discretion, which he said was the import of the
orders given him by Meade. A soldier's eye can
hardly be impressed with the stupendous weight of

General Sickles' discretion, in studying his old battle lines. Placing his right on the Emmetsburg Road at a point about three hundred yards southwest of the Codori House, which point was five or six hundred yards in advance of Hancock's left, he extended his line along the Emmetsburg Road for the distance of about a thousand yards, crossing the Wheatfield Road and going about one hundred yards beyond to the southwest corner of the Peach Orchard. At this point Sickles seemed to weaken in his determination to make the Emmetsburg Road his battle-line and rest his left on Seminary Ridge; for here he turned abruptly to the rearward, running thence at nearly a right angle with his former line in the direction of Little Round Top, which is distant from this point fully one mile in a direct line.

This, then, was the position of Sickles and the line he had selected. He had cut himself loose from the rest of the army; had isolated his corps; had taken up a position absolutely untenable, with his right five hundred yards in advance of his nearest

supports, and his centre advanced three-fourths of a mile beyond his supporting line; with his left, a long helter-skelter line of nearly a mile in extent, supported by nothing and resting nowhere. And this was the position in which Longstreet found him, when he opened the battle of July second.

CHAPTER XV

SICKLES' SALIENT

THE stars were shining brightly on the morning of the second of July, when I reported at General Lee's headquarters and asked for orders." Thus writes Longstreet, and thereby it seems that he was ready for active work in good season; but further on in his account he says: "General Lee was not ready with his plans," and, "as soon as it was light enough to see, the enemy was found in position on his formidable heights awaiting us." Then, Longstreet informs us, Lee sent an engineer to reconnoitre on his right, and also sent one of his staff to confer with Ewell as to the opportunity for making the battle by his left, and at ten o'clock "was still in doubt whether it would be better to move to his far-off right." It was Lee who was hesitating; but if he had not fully made up his mind to renew the battle against Meade's strong position when he surveyed the field from the cupola

moved his brigades down the Seminary Ridge and eastward in the shelter of the woods that covered all the lower reaches and slopes of this Confederate stronghold, so as to bring them in front of Humphrey's three brigades, which held the right of Sickles' line along the Emmetsburg Road. Sickles had begun to feel a trifle uneasy, all alone with his corps away out there close up to the woods on Seminary Ridge, and had thrown forward three battalions of sharpshooters — the First Vermont, First New York, and Third Maine — to develop the approaching enemy. Anderson's troops attacked and drove back these skirmishers; and General Birney, who commanded Sickles' left wing on his rearward line, reported this skirmish as beginning at eleven forty-five o'clock and ending at twelve fifty-five. From this field report we learn that at about one o'clock Anderson's brigades had full and complete possession of the woods that covered the eastern slope of Seminary Ridge in front of Sickles' right. Here they deployed, and Longstreet himself gives us the order of Anderson's formation, — "Wil-

cox's, Perry's, Wright's, Posey's, and Mahone's brigades from right to left." *

Away over the ridge there resided in 1900 a lady
who, as a little girl, lived in that vicinity at the time
of the battle. She stated to the writer in 1900, that
Longstreet's men were enthusiastic and boasted
that they had "whipped the stuffing" out of the
Yanks the day before, and would do the same thing
again before the sun went down. After passing beyond the point of Sickles' Salient, they crossed Seminary Ridge to the eastward in double lines. At the
crest of Seminary Ridge at the crossing or intersection of the Emmetsburg Road the Confederate
columns deployed for battle, McLaws' four brigades on the right of Anderson, in compact lines
fronting the point of the Salient; Hood's four brigades spreading out to the eastward, so as to envelop
Sickles' left, which was under the immediate command of Birney. Thus we find in the afternoon of
July second, the First Corps of the Confederate

---

* Longstreet's two divisions — McLaws' and Hood's —
marched to their positions by a route well concealed from
Sickles' view.

army away down the Valley of Gettysburg to the southward of Hancock's left flank, with the whole Confederate army in uninterrupted connection therewith, and in a position to move toward Washington and compel Meade to abandon his stronghold without a battle. All Lee had to do was to hold Longstreet in that threatening position while he concentrated his left and centre in that direction, and when night fell, to take up his line of march for the southward with Meade's army in the lurch. But surely Lee was looking for disaster, and not for victory, to such extent that he durst not draw away from the Hagerstown Road, which would afford him a safe retreat through the South Mountain passes to the Potomac. General Meade said that Sickles' position jeopardized his situation, in the fact that it brought on the battle before he was in readiness, and while twenty-eight thousand of his infantry and artillery were still absent; but really it seems to have had the opposite effect. The very boldness of Sickles' movement — his audacity in pushing his corps across the valley to within rifle-range of Seminary Ridge — was sufficient to give

Longstreet pause, and it is not strange that he believed the whole Army of the Potomac was in position behind him. With his line on Cemetery Ridge in connection with Hancock's left, Meade's position would have been in open view throughout, from the cupola of the Seminary; and having determined to give battle at eleven o'clock A.M. when he issued his battle-order, surely Lee would have seen to it that Longstreet moved at once to the attack; but away to the southward Sickles' Salient was screened by the almost overhanging woods of Seminary Ridge, while his left wing — Birney's whole division — was lost among the hills, groves, and ravines in the neighbourhood of Devil's Den and the Round Tops. Longstreet must have lost two precious hours in marching, counter-marching, and manœuvring for position. There was no vain show in the preparations for battle on either side. Sickles' regiments awaited the onset behind such hastily constructed cover as they could improvise, and his batteries occupied all the prominent knolls of commanding position, within and to the rearward of the Salient; while the Confederate artillery, far down

the Emmetsburg Road, bristled from every hill-top
and showed their gaping mouths from the wood-
screened heights of Seminary Ridge, as the long
lines of ragged butternut crept nearer and ever
nearer.

At last, late in the afternoon, Longstreet's brigades were in readiness. They were drawn close
around and confronting the Salient from the northwest, from the west, from the southwest, and from
the south. And here we will pause for a moment
while we take a last look at Sickles' Salient before
the battle opened. Could you, O reader, open an
immense pair of dividers at right angles, and lay
them upon that fair, diversified field, the point resting on the Emmetsburg Road one hundred yards
southwest of the crossing of the Wheatfield Road,
the left limb would lie along the Emmetsburg Road,
pointing toward Cemetery Hill, while the right limb
would point directly toward Little Round Top; but
while Humphreys' wing on the Emmetsburg Road
followed a ridge and was nearly straight throughout its length, Birney's wing, running in a generally
southeast direction, followed no ridge or defensive

line in particular, but was very crooked, doubling back and forth among the hills, swamps, and rocks, taking advantage of every position that afforded shelter and defence. Longstreet speaks of this locality as follows: "Hood's front was very rugged, with no field for artillery, and very rough for the advance of infantry."

Within this Salient the troops of the Third Corps had awaited battle for long hours on that July day, defiant of the gathering forces of the enemy, careless of increasing danger, ready to accept the chances of wounds and death; for was it not battle that Sickles, their General, courted and desired on that very ground, with all the chances of war against him ?

And where was Meade ? Where was the commanding General ? General Meade's headquarters were over the crest of Cemetery Ridge, two miles away to the northeast from the point of Sickles' Salient, just three hundred yards in rear of Hancock's right. In 1900, when the old veteran revisited the field, he followed Meade Avenue directly west from the old headquarters on the

GETTYSBURG

Taneytown Road to the crest of the ridge in the rear
of Hancock's position.   One hundred yards to the
right stands a steel tower of observation, erected at
this point on account of the prominence of its situation.   Fifty yards to the left or south of the tower,
stands a bronze equestrian statue of General Meade,
erected where the general commanding might be presumed to have stood, occasionally, when the lines
were forming for battle, and Longstreet was preparing his brigades and batteries to crush Sickles.
What a pity that General Meade did not ride forward from his headquarters, three hundred yards to
this sightly position, some time during the early part
of the second day of July, and with his field-glass
survey the valley away to the southwestward!   In
1900 the old veteran stood upon this ground, just
three hundred steps by actual count from General
Meade's headquarters, and saw, without a field-
glass, although his eyes were old, and dim with tears,
if not with age, the long line of white monuments
extending down the Emmetsburg Road to the old
Peach Orchard at Sickles' Salient, and thence southeastward along the hills, groves, glens, around the

loop, along the Wheatfield Road, and away to Devil's Den and Death Valley, which tell faintly the story of that terrible afternoon, and he said, over and over again, " Where was Meade ? "

And where were the members of Meade's staff ? Where were Hancock and his staff ? Is it the truth that from sunrise until three o'clock of July second, no man informed the commanding General, and General Meade did not know, that General Sickles, with his unsupported corps, was far away to the southwestward in an untenable position ?

It must have been an afterthought on Meade's part. While there was danger of Lee slipping away from his front, Meade was willing that Sickles should defy him and entice him to battle; but as the war-clouds thickened and battle became imminent, he was more than willing to saddle all the blame onto Sickles' shoulders. Along about three o'clock in the afternoon, however, Meade declared that in some unaccountable manner he made the discovery that Sickles had disregarded his instructions and formed his corps far out and away from the line that he had ordered him to occupy; and immediately he sent a despatch to Sickles, ordering him to withdraw his corps to Cemetery Ridge on Hancock's left; but it was too late — Longstreet was ready for battle, and had to be reckoned with in any further movement of troops on those lines that day. After the battle, General Meade talked in harsh terms of Sickles, and even essayed to prepare charges against him for disobedience of orders; but Sickles had lost a leg in the battle, and had fought like a hero, and Meade had really won a great victory, considering the chances against him in the beginning of the campaign, although at a tremendous cost; therefore Abraham Lincoln squelched the court-martial. Perhaps he thought that even if Sickles deserved punishment for forming his corps in such an indefensible position, the commanding General also deserved a greater degree of punishment for not knowing, in season to avert disaster, what his subordinate was doing while under his very eye; and if courts-martial were commenced, it would be hard to tell where they might end. Lincoln was generally not far from right.

CHAPTER XVI

THE old Peach Orchard of our war days was situated at the extreme apex of Sickles' Salient, on the east side of the Emmetsburg Road, and in the angle formed by its junction with the Wheatfield Road. Sickles' line on the Emmetsburg Road ended at the southwest corner of the Peach Orchard, there turning at a right angle to the eastward.

At about twenty minutes to four o'clock in the afternoon, Longstreet opened his batteries on that point, raking Sickles' lines with a withering cross-fire. His batteries, from commanding positions all along the Emmetsburg Road, away down to its intersection with Seminary Ridge, pounded the Peach Orchard and all within it most unmercifully, and swept, as with the besom of destruction, the whole length of Humphreys' wing. On the other hand, and at the same time, from over-topping heights on Seminary Ridge to the westward, not more than one-fourth of a mile away, other batteries poured down their cross-fire on the same devoted point and away and beyond, raking the length of Birney's wing, seeking out his infantry in their most secure hiding-places. However, Longstreet asserts that this cross-fire from the west hurt the right of his line, as well as Birney's; which was owing to the fact that beyond the Loop, Hood had drawn his lines so close, in an endeavour to strike Birney's flank, that the Confederate artillery fire from Seminary Ridge, intended for Birney's, passed beyond in part and disturbed Hood's infantry.

This strong artillery fire was continued for twenty minutes, and must have greatly shaken Sickles' infantry along both wings of his Salient. In the meantime Sickles' batteries were by no means idle, but their positions were less commanding. He had three batteries — C of the First New York, and C and F of the First Pennsylvania — in the Peach Orchard near the apex of his Salient and south of the Wheatfield Road, while on the north side of the road he had three others in proximity. He also had three batteries, the Fifth and the Ninth Massachusetts and the Tenth New York, planted on a prominent hill on the north side of the Wheatfield Road about three hundred yards east of its juncture with the Emmetsburg Road. Back of the Peach Orchard, which is situated on a plateau forming the top of the ridge, the country slopes rapidly but not precipitately to the eastward, forming a wide grassy valley that extends far away to the south. This valley divided Birney's line, his first brigade, commanded by Graham, being stationed west of it, in the Peach Orchard at the apex of the Salient, and a part of it facing to the westward in Humphreys' wing. This contour of the ground occasioned a wide gap in Birney's line, which beyond the valley was continued to the south and east at the beginning of the Loop, where De Trobriand's and Ward's brigades took it up and by devious ways, continued it in the direction of Devil's Den. The intervening valley is from two hundred and fifty to three hundred yards in width, and was not an inviting walk for Hood's troopers that July afternoon, as it was guarded at the upper end by the three last-named batteries — eighteen guns, with gaping mouths looking down its length from that commanding eminence, north of the Wheatfield Road.

During Longstreet's cannonade these last-named batteries were in a splendid position to return their compliments, and they were not allowing the time to pass in idleness; but the Confederate fire was intended to shake Sickles' infantry before the charging infantry lines swept forward to battle. At four o'clock the artillery fire slackened, and Longstreet's infantry, like a cyclone from out the South, struck Sickles' lines at the apex of his Salient, and the battle of Peach Orchard was on in all its fury. Longstreet's orders from Lee were: "Strike the enemy on his left flank and roll him up like a rubber blanket"; and there is no doubt that he did his best to carry out his instructions. The valley behind the Peach Orchard divided the combatants into two unequal parts. East of the valley Birney's two brigades maintained their position for a long time against Hood's four brigades; but the great struggle and the great battle for the first hour was in and around the Peach Orchard and along Humphreys' front, for the possession of the Emmetsburg Road. Longstreet's instructions from Lee were to keep close to the Emmetsburg Road and roll Sickles' line before him toward Cemetery Hill. To do that he had McLaws' division of his own and Anderson's division of Hill's corps — nine brigades in all — against Humphreys' four; and in less time than it takes to write it, the Confederate ranks surged around the Peach Orchard and far up the Emmetsburg Road, half concealed in sulphurous clouds fringed with flame. For the first hour it was almost exclusively Sickles' fight. It seemed for a long time that neither General Meade nor any one else was inclined to help Sickles out of his scrape; but Sickles was a fighter to be proud of, and no better soldiers ever lived than the men of the Third Corps. They were placed at a terrible disadvantage; they had been led like lambs to a slaughter-pen, but when the signal rang out for the slaughtering to begin they were lambs no longer, but first-class soldiers, and there was more or less slaughtering done on both sides.

The Third Corps did not "roll up," in compliance with Lee's programme, and it required all of Longstreet's ability as a general, and all the power and force of his "Great Rock," as he proudly called the First Corps, which he handled and bowled with consummate skill, to accomplish the job that he had undertaken. The apex of Sickles' Salient was so far away from Meade's main army and so out of joint with its harmonious formation, that it was impossible to render assistance in that quarter. If Sickles and his brave boys could not hold it alone and unaided, then surely it must be surrendered. The same condition presented itself with regard to Sickles' left flank, every part of that wing being fully a mile away from Hancock's farthest outpost, and in a locality broken and hilly. It was different with his right. Humphreys' wing occupied a strong position so far as his front was concerned, and with his flanks protected and made secure, he could have maintained his position against great odds; but his right was in the air, the ridge followed by the Emmetsburg Road falling away to a gentle swell at this point. The nearest troops in support of Humphreys' right was Hancock's line, six hundred yards to rearward; but straight up the Emmetsburg Road a mile away was the crest of Cemetery Hill, and along its western brow and all down the ridge to Hancock's right, every prominent knoll bristled with Meade's artillery. Within three hundred yards of the Emmetsburg Road, the farthest batteries not more than fifteen hundred yards from Humphreys' flank, thirty heavy guns commanded the valley. Then to the right of Hancock's line three infantry divisions — Doubleday's and Robinson's of the First, and Steinwehr's of the Eleventh Corps — guarded the west front of Cemetery Hill. Therefore there could have been no reasonable excuse for not protecting Humphreys' right. All the valley between the Emmetsburg Road and the ridge to the eastward was open and readily accessible to both infantry and artillery. Why should not a brigade and battery or two have been sent forward in season to make, at least, his right secure? Was the Commander-in-Chief so disturbed in his mind by what he seemed to regard as Sickles' wilfulness that he could not see his opportunity? Or may we not consistently inquire again, Where was Meade?

At all events, when the battle waxed heavy, Anderson swung his brigades on Humphreys' flank, rolling him back in some confusion, while the long-continued pounding broke in the apex of the Salient, and the whole right wing was forced back from the Emmetsburg Road. Far and wide the ridge was strewn with the dead, and the Peach Orchard was a slaughter-pen indeed!

The Third Corps was defeated and forced to a hasty retreat, but it was not yet out of the fight. Sickles had not chosen his lines at a venture and without due consideration. Almost from the apex of his Salient, the Wheatfield Road, like a central thoroughfare, ran eastward along the brow of the hill overlooking the valley that trended to the southward, and along that road his artillery found an open gateway to well-chosen positions of defence, selected for such an emergency with care and forethought before the battle opened, and back to the cover of rocks, hills, ravines, and woods, his well-seasoned regiments scurried away without loss of time.

Then, too, the discovery was at last made in the Union lines on Cemetery Hill that Sickles was really in trouble; and Hancock, either with or without orders from the Commander-in-Chief, sent forward Willard's brigade of his third division to reinforce Humphreys. But the battle of Peach Orchard was fought to a finish by the troops of the Third Corps alone, with no support from any source. Sickles made a mighty effort to hold back Longstreet's overpowering brigades, and always believed that it was the bold and defiant stand taken by him and the Third Corps that enticed Lee to turn from an open gateway to the southward, to beat out his brains against the rock-ribbed hills of Gettysburg, well manned by a determined but very anxious foe. The Third Corps backed their commander heroically. They believed, as he did, that the sacrifice was necessary, and they were willing to make it. The monuments and markers standing in sublime silence all down the Emmetsburg Road, beside the boundaries of the old Peach Orchard, in the angle of that unsupported far-away Salient, attest, and will forever attest to the determined fortitude and heroic patriotism of Dan Sickles and his Third Corps.

CHAPTER XVII

THE WHIRLPOOL OF BATTLE

AS Sickles' line fell back, his right and left wings were again united east of the valley trending southward from the Wheatfield Road, and guarded by his well-posted artillery during the former battle. As his Salient was reduced, his front was shortened and made more compact, thus serving to strengthen his line and improve his position.

Birney had been sore pressed and compelled to draw in his line at the Loop, also consolidating his front, which he still boldly presented to Hood's brigades. These movements established Sickles' second battle-line in a nearly north and south direction, from the western edge of the grove northeast of the Trostle House to Devil's Den, his centre being bent forward toward or near the Loop.

Longstreet had not succeeded in rolling Sickles up, but had forced him back fully half a mile, rather toward his left, into that uneven and broken region abounding in swales, ponds, ravines, gulches, rocks, thickets, and wooded hills.

It was a strange and singular location for the renewal of the battle, probably more uncertain for attack than for defence; but the afternoon was slipping away, — it was after five o'clock, — and if Longstreet intended to win a victory of any importance that day, he must press his brigades forward to their savage work.

Willard's brigade, coming fresh into the battle, struck the flank of Barksdale's advancing line with a furious fire, the movement being well supported by Humphreys' brigades, and soon the fighting became again most desperate and destructive. Captain Bigelow, commanding the Ninth Massachusetts Battery, had moved from his position on the Wheatfield Road overlooking the valley east of the Peach Orchard, taking up a new station about three hundred and fifty yards to the north and east of the former and just south of the Trostle House, where Sickles' headquarters were located. The battle for the possession of that point was pressed with great vigour by McLaws; and Bigelow remaining in his position until his supports were driven in, lost eighty horses out of eighty-eight. He was wounded himself, and lost six out of seven sergeants; but with the eight horses he had left he saved two out of six of his guns.

The battle on the left also became furious all along Birney's front from the Wheatfield Road to Devil's Den, Birney's splendid fighters utilizing every advantage of their grounds, hurling back their well-directed fire from depressions, rocks, trees, and stone fences. The Confederate General Hood was seriously wounded, and General Laws succeeded to the command of his division. General Semmes of McLaws' division, was mortally wounded. The Union General Willard, of Hancock's third division, was dead. General Sickles was terribly wounded. Still the battle thickened, and, if possible, increased in fury. Hancock sent forward Caldwell's whole division of four brigades, commanded by Cross, Kelly, Zook, and Brooke. Half of Hancock's corps was now in the battle, which was still unequal, and Longstreet pressed his advantage in numerical superiority, with the divisions of Law, McLaws, and Anderson, his eye on Cemetery Ridge as his goal of victory.

The sun was sinking toward the western mountains. The smoke of battle seemed to invite the early coming of night. Longstreet redoubled his efforts; he hurried every battery, every gun, into action; he pushed forward every regiment to the firing line.

Sickles was down and out, but the Third Corps, under Birney's leadership, was still doing heroic work, and Hancock was the guiding spirit of the Union battle, hurrying every gun and every man that he dared spare from his already weakened line at his right, out to the front in support of Birney, Humphreys, and Caldwell. About two-thirds of the distance from the apex of the Salient to Cemetery Ridge, and behind the hard-pressed Union line, there was an irregular plateau or open section of cultivated land called the Wheatfield. All around this field the country is rough, broken, and hilly; and along its eastern border Plum Run winds its course away to the southward, falling off precipitously into a rocky gorge that widens out, forming a deep valley between Little Round Top and Devil's Den opposite, about five hundred yards in a south of west direction.

This valley then trends to the southwestward, separating Devil's Den from Round Top, which sightly eminence stands slightly east of south therefrom, and about seven hundred yards distant. This valley between Devil's Den and Little Round Top and to the northward was named Death Valley from the carnage that took place therein that day.

From the low level of Death Valley to the eastward rises Little Round Top to the height of three hundred feet — a solid mass of boulders with scarcely a stunted shrub clinging to its rocky face. To the westward rises Devil's Den, to the height of from fifty to seventy feet, a solid mass of curiously carved and broken rocks of many acres in extent, adorned in places with clumps of stunted rock-oaks and other hardy shrubs. To the south rises Round Top to the height of six hundred feet — steep and very rocky; but, wonderful to relate, the pines and rock-oaks grow in luxuriance up to his very summit, making him both the king and the glory of the Gettysburg hills.

As the awful struggle of battle continued, Plum Run soon became Hancock's last line of defence west of Cemetery Ridge itself. Before the struggling Union forces lay the plateau of the Wheatfield; behind and above them, Cemetery Ridge. To occupy the ridge Longstreet must cross Plum Run; to cross Plum Run he must carry the plateau of the Wheatfield. To retain Cemetery Ridge until the arrival of reinforcements, Hancock must hold Plum Run; to hold Plum Run he must not allow Longstreet to pass the Wheatfield. Thus the struggle for the possession of the Wheatfield became the whole of the battle. On either side the lines were closely drawn. The Wheatfield, surrounded by hills and groves, broken with rocks, hedged in with stone walls, was transformed into a whirlpool more dreadful than Charybdis of olden times, more appalling than the Maelstrom of the North Sea.

At half-past five o'clock the battle lost all form of regularity. The lines swayed, twisted, surged, intermingled,—retreating, advancing, grappling, whirling, friend and foe in an irresistible vortex of war. Here we have the *quid obscurum* of Gettysburg, very similar to that portrayed by Hugo relative to the field of Waterloo — that portion of the battle unseen by mortal eye, so mixed, confused, and intricate that it never was and never can be understood.

In that savage and prolonged struggle, the contending armies within and around the Wheatfield seemed to assume formless and terrible proportions, more hideous and revolting than the prehistoric monsters that fought to their death in the deeps of the palæozoic ages of our infant world.

All around them the air became hot as from a furnace; above, the sky was obscured with clouds of sulphurous smoke; the sun was veiled and fled in haste toward the shelter of the western mountains. The earth trembled; the rocks were overturned; the hills shook beneath their violent contortions. The valleys and fields ran red with the blood of their carnage.

The Confederate general, Barksdale, was dying. G. L. Anderson, of Laws' division, was wounded.

General Zook, of Hancock's first division, was dead. Brooke was wounded. Cross was dying. Through it all the Confederate war-monster seemed more powerful than his antagonist, gaining the ascendency over the Union war-monster and crowding him back slowly, but surely and continuously.

At twenty minutes past six o'clock the situation of the Union army was desperate. If Lee did not support Longstreet with reinforcements from his centre and left, as Longstreet complained bitterly that he did not, what can be said of Meade ? What did the Commander-in-Chief of the Union army do to relieve the tension ? If it is true that Lee was asleep, or had forgotten his "old war horse," as he sometimes called Longstreet, in the stress of the mightiest effort of his life, is it not also true that Meade came very near forgetting Hancock in his desperate struggle to maintain his position ? To the right of Hancock's line many batteries, and three divisions, or seven brigades of Union infantry defended the west front of Cemetery Hill; and two of those brigades had hardly pulled a trigger in the battle of the previous day. They were not under

Hancock's command, and Meade did not feel warranted in weakening the line by a single regiment, although the position was naturally so rugged and strong that a skirmish line could have held it against a line of battle. At least he did not. It was not Longstreet against the Army of the Potomac; but up to that moment and until half an hour later, it was Longstreet's three divisions, comprising thirteen brigades, against Hancock's and Birney's three divisions, comprising eleven brigades, so that the weight of battalia was with Longstreet.

But now the time had arrived when it became necessary for Meade, the commanding General of the Union army, to make some movement on the chess-board of war; for surely and certainly it was the danger hour, not alone for the Army of the Potomac, but for the American Republic as well. Since the birth of the nation there was never an hour fraught with danger more imminent. The life of the nation was in the balance. Two hours before, Meade had received a despatch from Sedgwick, informing him that the Sixth Corps was on the march and doing its utmost to reach the field.

About the same time a despatch from Sykes informed him that the Fifth Corps was nearer by several miles than the Sixth. The afternoon was desperately hot; the men of the Fifth Corps were not made of asbestos, but what humanity could they would do. It is not recorded of Meade that, as he watched and waited during those anxious hours, he was heard to murmur, " Sykes or night !" but more than likely that prayer was in his heart.

At twenty minutes past six o'clock the vanguard of the Fifth Corps was not yet in sight, and Meade could wait no longer for their coming. Then he sent a despatch to Slocum that imperilled the right but did not relieve the left. It showed Meade's good intentions, however, which were worth something, and if he did more than mean well, history has failed to make a record of it. The despatch to Slocum called for reinforcements. Slocum sent him Lockwood's brigade of his first division, but as the call was most urgent, Slocum concluded to take some chances; so, hastily turning his whole line over to the care of General Greene and his third brigade of the second division, with instructions to extend a skirmish line to replace his line of battle from the crest of Culp's Hill to Rock Creek, and if attacked, to hold the whole line as long as possible; and when the battle became too heavy, to retire to the crest and hold that citadel forever. Slocum marched away to the left with the balance of the Twelfth Corps, leaving one brigade — a mere skirmish line — to hold Culp's Hill and its important slopes against Johnson's division of four brigades. It was a daring and perilous movement, one of the mighty risks of war that sometimes must be taken.

CHAPTER XVIII

GENERAL G. K. WARREN, chief of engineers on General Meade's staff, may truthfully be called the saviour of Little Round Top; and for his work that day he earned the everlasting gratitude of his country; but without a heroic effort on the part of others, no man could have saved it; and the key to our left, as Little Round Top certainly was, would have fallen into the hands of the Confederates.

Along in the afternoon, when the battle was raging fiercely to the westward, General Warren rode far down Cemetery Ridge, ascended that knob of boulders, and established on the summit thereof a signal station. The eastern and northern faces of Little Round Top, though steep and rocky, are not nearly so high and difficult of ascent as the western face from Death Valley. Warren soon made the

[185]

discovery that the bold knob on which he stood was a most important position — not for the Union army while it remained unoccupied by the Confederates, as it then was; but if it were once in their possession and crowned with their artillery, they could enfilade the entire length of Cemetery Ridge and take Meade's position in reverse from Cemetery Hill to Rock Creek. Yet there was not a Union soldier there to defend it, except Warren and two or three men of the Signal Corps. Then, as the afternoon wore away and the battle drew nearer, increasing in fury around the Wheatfield, Warren made the further discovery that Laws had his eye on Little Round Top; and as he looked he saw a flanking column moving out from Devil's Den across Plum Run valley, headed directly for the knob of boulders on which he stood. A message to signal headquarters at Cemetery Hill could bring no timely relief even if a regiment could be spared for that purpose, as the distance was more than two miles, and within half an hour the advancing Confederates would be in possession without firing a gun. But there were defenders nearer; at that moment Warren's ears caught the sound of marching troops, and the vanguard of the Fifth Corps, so anxiously looked for by Meade and Hancock, appeared on the Taneytown Road not four hundred yards in rear of the threatened position.

Never in the history of war was arrival more timely. The advent of Blucher's army on the field of Waterloo was not more opportune to the exhausted English than was Sykes' corps to Warren and the exhausted troops of Hancock and Birney. A further delay of half an hour for any cause, and Sykes would have found Little Round Top in Laws' possession, and Cemetery Ridge occupied by Longstreet and his Confederates. The Army of the Potomac would have been split into two frag-ments, the Fifth and Sixth Corps out of the battle, and Lee master of the situation.

Had Longstreet begun his battle two hours earlier, — at two rather than at four o'clock, — it would have been over before Sykes' arrival, and the Battle of Gettysburg would have been counted as the most terrible defeat of the Union cause. Lee's unaccountable hesitation and unreadiness in the morning; Sickles' daring and defiant Salient that puzzled Longstreet and delayed his attack; the stubborn resistance and heroic endurance of the Third Corps — all combined to bring a far-reaching victory to the Union cause at the bloody sunset hour. Warren hurried down over the rocks to the point where he had left his horse, and rode in haste to the marching column, detaching Vincent's brigade of the first division, which he hurried to the summit of Little Round Top just in time to meet Laws' brigade of Alabamans climbing its western face, and they drove back the Southern men into the valley. In this struggle the gallant Vincent was mortally wounded. Tilton's and Sweitzer's brigades of Sykes' corps were hurried to the front to reinforce the Second and Third Corps. Then out of the former chaos the battle along the eastern verge of the Wheatfield began to assume form and regularity. The first and second brigades of the second division, and also the third division of two brigades of the Fifth Corps, followed in support of the main battle, meeting with a withering fire Longstreet's temporarily victorious brigades that had won the

Wheatfield and were advancing toward the crest of Cemetery Ridge.

But Laws had not yet abandoned his design on Little Round Top; and Benning's brigade of Georgians having reinforced the Alabamans, they tried again to carry the hill of boulders. General Weed with the third brigade of the second division of the Fifth was then ordered to reinforce and hold Little Round Top. Colonel O'Rorke, with the One Hundred and Fortieth New York Infantry, was the first to reach the firing line in support of Vincent's brigade, and a hand-to-hand conflict raged again on the slippery rocks and declivities. By order of Weed, Hazlett's battery (D of the Fifth U. S. Artillery) was by hand and with ropes dragged to the summit; but the Confederate sharpshooters, located behind the boulders of Devil's Den, picked off the Union artillerymen so rapidly as to render their guns of little or no service for a time. General Weed was mortally wounded; and while Hazlett was leaning over him, receiving his dying message, he also was hit, and fell dead across Weed's body.

GETTYSBURG

We have had occasion heretofore to speak of the expert marksmanship of the Confederate soldiers, but on no field of the war did they exhibit greater skill in that capacity than at this time and place. The rocks of Devil's Den are certainly five hundred yards, and probably more, from the summit of Little Round Top; but across the yawning chasm of Plum Run they made life uncertain for the Union soldiers who guarded it. The Confederates, however, had one great advantage over their opponents. They were shooting upward, and the boulders of Little Round Top were aglow with the rays of the setting sun. The Union soldiers stood out against the sky clear and distinct to their eyes, a shining mark for their dexterity; while the superior quality of their powder must also be taken into consideration.

On the other hand, the Union soldiers were looking downward, into an abyss, as it were, with the dazzling sunshine in their eyes, and the marks at which they directed their shots indistinct, within the shadow of overhanging rocks. Nevertheless a company or two of Berdan's sharpshooters were hastily distributed among the rocks and crevices, and they soon returned the Confederate fire with satisfactory effect; and as the sun went down behind the South Mountain, giving to each party of distant combatants a fair and equal chance, the Union artillery was brought into play upon their rocky stronghold, with the result that, when the battle was over, many a Georgian, and many an Alabaman, was found among the rocks of Devil's Den who never retreated, not a few bearing no mark of ball or shell, but killed by the concussion of shell or solid-shot against the rocks upon which they depended for protection.

So Little Round Top was held and made secure, but the battle did not cease with the going down of the sun; for half an hour later it was raging terrifically in Death Valley and along the Wheatfield plateau. The stone walls and rocky defences on the east side of the Wheatfield were recaptured, as was also Devil's Den, and held by the Union forces. At eight o'clock the battle ceased. Longstreet says: "While Meade's lines were growing, my men were dropping; we had no others to call to their aid, and the weight against us was too heavy to carry. The sun was down, and with it went down the severe battle." That statement is true. During the sunset hour the weight of battalia was against Longstreet.

The Fifth Corps entered the arena at about seven o'clock. It comprised eight brigades, and numbered 12,500 men; but as the afternoon was terribly hot and the corps had marched steadily and rapidly, if it went into the battle with twelve thousand men it made a splendid record. A reinforcement of twelve thousand fresh soldiers (for although weary enough with marching and nearly exhausted with excessive heat, they were fresh in comparison with the men who had been hours in battle) to a battle-line originally but eighteen thousand strong, and that had lost thousands, is a great addition to its battle strength. Thus the Union army, starting in with Sickles' corps of twelve thousand, was reinforced after the first hour with six thousand, and again at seven o'clock with twelve thousand, making its battle strength at the finish nineteen brigades and 30,000 men, less the loss of the day; while

GETTYSBURG

Longstreet made the battle without reinforcements, but from start to finish with thirteen brigades and 26,000.

On the whole it was not so very unequal. Longstreet says: "My loss was about six thousand, Meade's between twelve and fourteen thousand." It is useless at this point to discuss the Confederate losses; but Longstreet's estimate of the Union losses is greatly exaggerated. Assuming that the Third Corps' entire loss of 4,198 was sustained on the second of July, and also the Fifth Corps' entire loss of 2,186, to the sum of which we add half the entire loss of the Second Corps, which cannot be far from a correct estimate, and it brings the aggregate loss of the Union army on July second up to about 9,000, which is more than forty per cent in excess of Longstreet's loss as he estimates it.

But whatever the battle losses of the second of July may have been, it was the decisive battle of the series, and bloody enough to satisfy any votary of war and carnage.

It must have been about seven o'clock when the

first shots were fired by Vincent's brigade of the Fifth Corps on Little Round Top. Within a few minutes thereafter, every brigade and every regiment of that twelve thousand men were in the fire and fury of battle, where they remained to the end of the struggle. One hour only, one hour at the going down of the sun, and until darkness overshadowed the earth, and yet in that short space of time, the Fifth Corps sustained a loss of more than two thousand men. Was there ever a bloodier sunset hour?

After dark Meade ordered the withdrawal of his lines from all points westward to the ridge, extending an unbroken line from Cemetery Hill to Round Top; and Sickles made no objection, being content to let his " Salient " go with his leg.

Before seeking his couch that night it is said that Lee on bended knees offered up thanks to God on high for what Longstreet had so dearly won; and Meade returned thanks to the same wise Providence for what Longstreet had failed to win; while the whole Army of the Potomac thanked God indeed for the timely arrival of the Fifth Corps; and all the people of the United States thanked Him, and the boys of the Third, Second, and Fifth Corps for their heroic fighting, done all along the line.

CHAPTER XIX

CEMETERY HILL AND CULP'S HILL

THE battles of July second began, but did not end with Peach Orchard, nor yet with the Wheatfield and Little Round Top. Lee had determined to try the strength of the centre and the right, as well as of the left of the Union army that day; but Longstreet affirms that all other movements were dilatory and untimely.

The fact that the left did not " roll up," as readily as Lee anticipated, caused him, no doubt, somewhat to change his programme. Still, he had his eye on both the other points, and before the battle entirely ceased on the left, both the centre and the right came in also for a touch of war.

Between Cemetery Hill and the western prolongation of Culp's Hill there is a narrow valley extending southward in a deep indentation, and thence rising gently by a grassy slope, thus separating the two elevations as it passes upward. Running along the northeastern base of Cemetery Hill from Baltimore Street, a narrow lane leads up this valley to the point where Slocum Avenue now crosses it from hill to hill. That lane was there on July second, and along its southern side extended an old but well preserved and strong stone wall, forming a splendid breastwork for infantry. Behind this stone wall were posted a part of Howard's Eleventh Corps, comprising Ames' and Von Gilsa's brigades. North of this valley Early's division of Ewell's corps held the Confederate line. Above and behind Howard's brigades Cemetery Hill fairly gleamed with guns, whose gaping mouths commanded the valley and line, and from West Culp's Hill Stevens' Fifth Maine Battery, which did such splendid service on Seminary Ridge in the battle of July first, looked savagely down from its commanding position.

At the foot of Culp's Hill and about a dozen yards northeast from the lane, is a large spring from which a ravine trends easterly toward Rock Creek. Both the lane and ravine afforded protection to advancing troops until well within this valley; and just outside of it Early had massed his division for a desperate effort to capture Cemetery Hill. Just after sunset of July second the crash of musketry in the valley below announced to the men at their guns on Cemetery Hill and Culp's Hill that the battle was on.

Longstreet gives the time of Early's attack at nine o'clock P.M. but it certainly occurred much earlier. Even then it is hard to account for the fact that it was not made earlier than it was, with a heavier column and in concert with the height of the battle on our left. An attack on a strong position after sunset by two brigades seems but foolishness. Early's two brigades had crept up the lane and ravine under cover of the gathering darkness, as far as they could possibly go without attracting the attention of Howard's troops, and then, with Hayes' brigade of Louisiana Tigers in the lead, supported by Hoke's North Carolina brigade, charged straight for Howard's line of infantry, yelling and firing as they advanced with a rush.

Howard's infantry seemed to have been caught napping. Their line was too near the foot of the hill, and Early's men were almost on them before they were discovered. This made it impossible for the artillery to get into action, as they would rake friend and foe alike. Howard's regiments returned the fire, but the attack was so sudden, and the Confederates charged with such impetuous determination that they soon gave way before the rush of the fiery Tigers from the canebrakes of Louisiana. Those Louisiana men paid no heed to musketry or bayonets, but dashed through all opposition, and swarming over the stone wall and up the slope, captured two guns of Rickett's battery and fought hand-to-hand with the gunners for the others. But the artillery boys fought desperately with stones, sponge-staffs, and rammers, when they could not use their guns, holding their ground like heroes. Finally, Early's line had advanced so far up the hill that their left flank was turned for a moment in the direction of the guns of the Fifth Maine Battery on the western spur of Culp's Hill, which raked them fore and aft with canister. At the same moment Battery B of the Fourth U. S. Artillery gave them canister in front at short range. Nothing human could withstand such a reception for any length of time, and they soon fell back to shelter. A moment later the infantry line was reinforced by Carroll's brigade of Hancock's third division (for Hancock was our watchman on the wall that day), which dashed down the slope of Cemetery Hill, clearing both lane and ravine.

This was Early's last and only attempt to climb Cemetery Hill; and there many of his brave followers found a last home. Of the Tigers who led the charge, less than seven hundred returned to their lines, and the organization was about wiped from existence. It was a bold and desperate effort, but, for the Confederates, a most discouraging failure.

This battle was of short duration, but exceedingly sharp while it lasted. Carroll's brigade lost about one hundred men, while Ames and Von Gilsa together lost about four hundred, or five hundred in all. The Confederate loss was severe, the Tigers alone losing more than our entire loss.

Simultaneously with Early's attempt to carry Cemetery Hill, Johnson's second division of

Ewell's corps, which held the extreme left of Lee's line, made a vigourous, determined, and for a time successful attack on the extreme Union right on Culp's Hill, held by Slocum's Twelfth Corps.

Culp's Hill was the strongest natural position along our whole line, with the possible exception of Little Round Top. It is a high, rocky hill, with a sharp ridge extending southeastward from its point of highest elevation nearly to Rock Creek, a distance of about a mile. The western prolongation adjoining the Eleventh Corps was held by the old veteran's division, commanded by General Wadsworth of the First Corps. This was joined on the right by Slocum's corps, which extended the Union line to Rock Creek and beyond. The hill itself is a tower of strength, and the face of the ridge to the north and eastward is abrupt and easily defended; but as it nears Rock Creek it slopes away more gradually, ending in a level meadow about three hundred yards wide, along which winds the stream. Back and southward of this ridge a small branch heads in the valley west of the Baltimore Pike, which runs eastwardly, crossing the pike, flowing into Rock Creek east of the termination of the ridge.

Spangler's Spring, a natural fount of water, is situated just back of the easternmost prolongation of the ridge, and about fifty yards north of the branch, with which it is connected by a streamlet. These valleys uniting at this point make a wide open space; it lay at Slocum's right, penetrating far to rearward, which required to be guarded carefully. While the battle was in progress on the left of Meade's line and around the Wheatfield at the danger hour, as we have seen, Slocum was called to reinforce the left with every man he could spare from his line. Slocum had in his corps 8,589 men to hold a line a mile long and guard the valley and creek on his right, and it was this line that he left to the care of Greene with only one brigade.

Johnson's division of Ewell's corps, with four brigades, held the Confederate line opposite; and when Johnson discovered the weakness of Slocum's or Greene's line he prepared at once to capture it, but was late in making the attack. When he did, Greene's skirmish line made it lively for him for

some time. Johnson finally swept in along the creek
and carried the ridge northward for the distance of
about nine hundred yards, Greene's men retiring
before him to the crest, which they held. The Second Maryland Confederate Infantry penetrated up
the ridge to the farthest point occupied by any of
Johnson's forces; their monument stood close up to
the crest with monuments of the Union regiments
when the old veteran visited the field, showing the
exact division point of the contending forces during
the night of July second. This monument of the
Second Maryland was the only Confederate monument allowed to be placed on the Union line at that
time; and shows that all the ridge below it, down to
Rock Creek, was held that July night by Johnson's
Confederates.

Johnson then left part of his division to hold the
ridge against Greene, and, with the balance, moved
cautiously up the valley of the branch in rear of
Culp's Hill, as far as the Baltimore Pike, without
meeting any opposition. Four hundred yards
farther and just north of Power's Hill was parked
Meade's whole reserve ammunition and supply

train, but Johnson did not know it. It was after dark. The battle was over; not a shot was being fired, and Johnson really became alarmed. To his staff he said: "This is too easy; I believe the Yanks have set a trap for us." So he marched his troops back to Slocum's vacant line on the ridge, and reunited his division, where he camped and waited for morning.

Slocum's corps did not get into the battle on the left, only a regiment or two of Lockwood's brigade having taken places to strengthen Hancock's line. The Fifth Corps arrived before the Twelfth, and Slocum hastened back to secure his imperilled position. As he marched slowly along, picking his way in the darkness, he was not many minutes in rear of Johnson's retiring troops, and when he arrived at the branch in rear of the ridge he found his lines occupied by the Confederates in force. Slocum camped his corps along the south side of the branch, with Spangler's Spring between his lines and Johnson's. The night was sultry. The soldiers on both sides were famished for water. The water in the streams was warm as the heat of a July sun could make it. So the soldiers, who were to engage in mortal strife at the first peep of dawn, drew their supply of water, far into the night, in peace from Spangler's Spring.

CHAPTER XX

AGAIN merciful night spread his mantle over the battlefield. The dead slept in peace, the wounded suffered and endured, and the living and well prepared for the morrow and the renewal of the sanguinary struggle.

The Sixth Corps under the command of Sedgwick, 15,555 strong, arrived on the field almost before the battle of the second day had ceased, thus at last concentrating and reuniting the Army of the Potomac in its full strength and completeness; and from that moment Lee's last chance for the realization of his ambitious dream was at an end.

While the Union army had lost 18,000 men during the previous two days of battle, it would confront Lee on the morrow with an unbroken front four miles long; with 65,000 men in line and on reserve; with its left buttressed on Round Top and its right upon Culp's Hill; but a leader for the hour and the occasion was not there. Defensively, Meade's position was impregnable. The temporary lodgment of Johnson on the southeastern spur of Culp's Hill could be readily overcome, while on his flanks were his cavalry, active and watchful, ready to grapple with and turn back Stuart on his approach from either direction.

Offensively, Meade had already abandoned the idea, if he ever entertained it. Lee held the Hagerstown and the Emmetsburg Roads, with a wide open door for retreat the moment the necessity should arrive; and Meade would never attempt to cut his army in two or crush his right in order to get possession of that back-door. The man who was to fight Lee to a finish and bar the door behind him was yet to be found.

So General Meade prepared to stay, and in that he did well; but the idea of capturing or destroying Lee's army never entered his head. He strengthened his lines from Culp's Hill to Round Top, throwing up entrenchments in the weak places, that are still there, and planting batteries in every available position.

GETTYSBURG

It was now Lee's turn to call a council of war. It had been wiser to call a council of retreat, but the retreat came in due season, with or without a council. At the council Lee was still the master spirit, the same indomitable and courageous leader; in fact, at this council more than at any other time in his life, Lee laid himself open to the charge of mulishness. He would listen to no change of his plan of procedure. He said to his corps commanders and generals there assembled, "To-morrow I will assault Meade's centre."

To this Longstreet objected; he said, "General Lee, we have failed to-day in a mighty effort to break Meade's front or turn his left. I give it as my opinion that another effort cannot succeed. I would advise moving southward by the Emmetsburg Road, which is now clear, toward Washington, thus compelling Meade to abandon his stronghold and give us battle on more favourable ground."

Lee replied: "No, gentlemen! No! I will strike him between the eyes. I have to-night been reinforced by Pickett's division of infantry, the flower of my army, and by Stuart's cavalry."

GETTYSBURG

Here it becomes necessary to diverge from the proceedings of Lee's war-council and explain the cause and manner of these reinforcements just received by Lee's army. Pickett's division of infantry was the second division of Longstreet's corps, and comprised three brigades, all Virginians; the first, commanded by Garnett, consisting of five Virginia regiments; the second, commanded by Kemper, consisting also of five Virginia regiments; the third, commanded by Armistead, of five Virginia regiments; making a complete division of Virginia troops — fifteen regiments in all. Lee, himself a Virginian, was extremely partial to Virginian troops. Lee's partiality to Virginians created some jealousy in his army, expressed by the saying, common among his officers, "Too much Virginia." But the rank and file really had no reason to complain of the high esteem in which he held Pickett's division, in contemplation of the honour he designed bestowing upon them the following day. Pickett's division had been left at Chambersburg under orders from headquarters, to guard trains; and during the battles of the first and second of July they got more enjoyment out of Lee's invasion of Pennsylvania than they did afterwards.

Stuart's cavalry comprised five brigades, commanded by Wade Hampton, Fitzhugh Lee, W. H. F. Lee, Robertson, and Jones, with six batteries of horse artillery under the command of Beckham. On crossing the Potomac, Lee had left Stuart behind to befog Hooker as long as possible; then to cross the Potomac and ride east toward Baltimore, in order to draw the Union cavalry from the route of travel designed for the Confederate supply trains. Following these instructions Stuart made a complete circuit of the Union army, riding hard to no purpose except to jade and weary his horses and men. This was another and very serious mistake of Lee in his campaign of invasion, for it deprived him of the use of the main body of his cavalry up to the last day of the battle. As a general's cavalry are his eyes, Lee was like unto the blind Samson feeling for the pillars of the temple of Dagon. This absence of Stuart disturbed Lee's mind greatly, and was one of the causes for his loss of balance.

GETTYSBURG

As Longstreet says, "It may, with the success of the first day, have moved him to make precipitate battle as his safest means of escape." Knowing that Lee's original destination was Harrisburg, Stuart headed that way, and on June thirtieth he encountered Kilpatrick's division of Union cavalry in the town of Hanover, fourteen miles east of Gettysburg. Stuart was not then looking for a fight, but anxious to reach Lee's army; so he hastily retreated from Hanover toward Carlisle, where he arrived on the evening of July first. There he learned that Lee had abandoned his contemplated attack on Harrisburg, left the Cumberland Valley, crossed to the east side of the South Mountain, and that there had already been one day's fighting between his army and the Army of the Potomac at Gettysburg. From Carlisle, Stuart rode southward and reached Lee's army at Gettysburg on the evening of July second.

Therefore, in that war-council Lee said: "I have been reinforced by Pickett's division of infantry, and Stuart's cavalry. To-morrow morning I will mass Pickett's division in the woods on the west slope of Seminary Ridge, in front of Meade's left centre, well supported to the right and left. I will despatch Stuart around Meade's right flank to make a rear attack in conjunction with Pickett's attack from the front; then shall every battery and every gun along our entire line open and concentrate their fire upon that point in Meade's line, the centre of which is designated by that umbrella-shaped clump of trees, that shall mark Pickett's objective; and when the bombardment shall cease, then shall Pickett and Stuart charge, and I will cut Meade's army in two, and afterwards destroy it in detail." Too late! too late! The Army of the Potomac was united, and there was no power on earth except that of Almighty God that could cut it in two, or defeat it where it stood.

It would seem, however, that God Almighty, if He stoops to interfere in battles of men more than in common dog-fights, was directing Lee's plan for a purpose. All Confederate accounts agree that up to that time the Union battle-loss had been much greater than theirs. If Lee was strong enough to invade the North, he was, comparatively, stronger and better able to continue the invasion. His army was also united, and he had with him his cavalry, which he had so greatly needed. If he was strong enough to risk another effort against such a position as the Union army occupied, he was certainly strong enough to slip away from Meade's front, down the valley toward Washington. What a surprise it would have been to Meade, who dreaded the offensive as Satan dreads the sunlight! But it surely would have been up to him to move quickly and skilfully to avoid the onus of battle for the security of the national capital.

By that movement, what an opportunity would have been presented to Lee to put in practice his skilful generalship, that had served him so well on many occasions! But he elected to forego all his strategic ability and wise daring, and to stand inert on Seminary Ridge while his devoted followers took another buck at the rock-ribbed hills, more than a mile out of their way.

We have no fault to find with the unseen and unknown powers that directed the conclusion of that council. Whether it was the spirit of God, or of old John Brown, that weighed down Lee's soul, or whether he used his best judgment untrammelled by all prejudicial influences, the world in general and the people of the United States in particular are justified in thanking God; for it resulted in the preservation of the Union.

CHAPTER XXI

DURING the night of July second, Slocum prepared his thunderbolt of war, to be launched early in the morning of the third, for the right had now become the danger-point in Meade's line. Culp's Hill or Ridge, was the only point where the great high tide of the Rebellion, which surged and beat so savagely against the Union lines on the afternoon of July second, found a lodgment. The wave still remained on Culp's Ridge, firmly fixed in the form of Johnson's Confederate division of four brigades — eight thousand men. That night another Confederate wave rolled in and mingled with the first, adding to its strength.

The second wave of the Confederate tide rolled in very gently during the night in the form of three additional brigades — Smith's from Early's, and Daniel's and O'Neal's from Rodes' division.

This wave gave Johnson twelve thousand men; and there certainly seemed to be a chance for a strong aggressive battle on Slocum's part for the repossession of his old line along the ridge. Why Ewell did not send the other three brigades of Rodes' division, and especially Gordon's brigade of Early's, is, to say the least, passing strange. Gordon was the man who was anxious (so he said) to climb those heights with his brigade alone on the evening of July first. Surely he would have enjoyed slipping up there in the night time with friends already there to greet him, and no enemy there to meet him before morning; but both Ewell and Lee failed to see their opportunity.

As Lee was determined to fight the battle out on that line, he might have greatly improved his chances of success by concentrating his forces on his left where he had a footing, and charging Meade's position from the rear, instead of from the front. Culp's Ridge is almost directly in the rear of Hancock's and Doubleday's positions, which Lee made his mad effort to carry from their front; and the distance is not so great, while the ground is uneven and affords much protection for advancing infantry. The only reason that can be imagined why Lee preferred to let his opportunity in rear of Culp's Hill and the Union lines go by default, after it was fairly and almost bloodlessly in his possession, was his certainty of disaster and his fear to uncover the Hagerstown Road through the mountain passes, his road home to Virginia.

However, Meade seemed to have had small fear for his right. He massed in reserve two divisions of the Sixth Corps in proximity to Slocum's lines, apparently regarding Slocum as perfectly competent to accomplish the work entrusted to him. He sent him Shaler's brigade from the Sixth Corps, which increased Slocum's force to a trifle over ten thousand men, or seven brigades against Johnson's seven; but Greene's brigade, it must be remembered, held the summit or Culp's Hill proper, and, as situated, was worth any other two brigades for attack or defence. Slocum formed Geary's division and Shaler's brigade in the valley facing the ridge to the northeast, while he massed Ruger's division on Geary's right, extending to Rock Creek.

The brigades of both Slocum and Johnson were ready for action very early in the morning of July third. Each army tried to assume the initiative. Johnson had his lines formed and was about to open the attack on Slocum's position in the valley when Slocum's batteries on Power's Hill, a prominent eminence to the southward near the Baltimore Pike, opened fire on Johnson's lines above the heads of Slocum's troops, while at the same time Greene's batteries opened from the summit of Culp's Hill enfilading the whole length of Johnson's position down the ridge. This severe cannonading threw the Confederates into great confusion, compelling them to seek shelter and re-formation. Again they advanced, when in addition to the artillery cross-fire, Geary's division met them with a withering fire of musketry; and Greene's brigade, from their commanding perch, raked the ridge as far down as their pieces would carry. It was a hot place for the Confederates, but they stood bravely to their work, returning the Union musketry-fire in true Southern style; but they were at a great disadvantage in the use of artillery. They had some batteries on Wolf's

Hill, east of Rock Creek, but the trend of the ridge whereon their infantry was stationed protected Geary's line. Ruger's division, farther to the right, along and near the creek, was more exposed.

Thus the battle raged fiercely for hours, each side losing heavily, and clinging to its purpose tenaciously. About nine o'clock the Second Maryland Confederate Infantry, that held the highest point attained on the hill by Johnson's men, made a bold and desperate attempt to storm the summit of the hill above them and thus get possession of the commanding citadel; but they were repulsed with heavy loss. Their colonel was wounded and captured, and the regiment lost fifty per cent of its number.

About half-past nine o'clock Ruger's division swung around to the right, taking Johnson's line in the flank, rolling them up the ridge toward the northwest in grand shape. Johnson made a heroic effort to retain possession of the ridge he had won so easily the night before, but Ruger's charge was too impetuous, and he abandoned the ridge with the loss of five hundred prisoners, and many killed and wounded, retreating helter-skelter through the woods to the shelter of the thickets in the valley. By ten o'clock Slocum had won a complete victory, reëstablishing his lines where he had planted them on the night of July first, the Confederates thereafter making no further demonstration against the Union right.

In this battle, which was distinctly separate from any other and a continuation of the battle of Culp's Hill of July second, Slocum's corps lost 1,082 men, to which may be added the loss of seventy-five from Shaler's brigade of the Sixth Corps, increasing Slocum's total loss in the battle to 1,157. Johnson's division lost 1,821, to which must be added the loss sustained by Smith's, Daniel's, and O'Neal's brigades, in order to ascertain Johnson's full loss. This is one battle wherein the Confederates certainly outnumbered the Union troops, and also wherein the Confederate records show a greater loss than that sustained by the Union forces.

Lee seemed to have perfect confidence in his plan of battle for July third, as previously portrayed to his generals in their war-council, by which he

expected to cut Meade's army in two and defeat
it utterly.

The supposition expressed by some historians,
that Lee ordered Pickett's Charge, as the main battle of July third is called, not with the expectation
of breaking the Union centre, but simply to gain
time — as a kind of bluff, to deter Meade from making an offensive or counter movement on his lines
while his army was preparing to retreat — is at
variance with every known fact and movement in
connection with his army during July third.

There was no bluff about it, and no necessity for
a bluff. Lee well knew that there would be nothing
"offensive" about Meade, whatever the result of
his final effort to break his lines; otherwise he never
would have taken the desperate risk of sending
Stuart's jaded cavalry on another wide circuit and
wild dash, wherein he was expected to try titles with
a line of securely posted infantry; nor would he
have put his only division of infantry that had not
been war-hammered and terribly battered within
the previous two days and on which he might rely

as a reserve in some emergency that might occur, into the fiercest hell of battle; where, if it failed of success, the result must be the certain and complete destruction of the whole division.

Lee still hoped that the star of his fortune had not deserted him; that God, or good luck, was with him and at last would give him the victory. In this he was sadly mistaken, but he knew of a certainty that the gateway behind him was always open for his retreat to the Potomac and into Virginia, and that Meade would make no effort worthy of the name to close that gate against him or wrench it from his possession, even if Stuart and all his cavalry rode beyond the shadow of everlasting night, and the last man of Pickett's division lay stark and cold on the death-haunted field.

So Lee issued his orders for the day's operations, and very early in the morning, before Johnson and Slocum had joined battle, Stuart was in the saddle leading his daring riders in a wide detour around the right flank of the Union army.

Three and a half miles east of Gettysburg, where certain cross-roads, leading southward beyond

Wolf's Hill toward the Baltimore Pike, intersect the Hanover Road, Stuart encountered Gregg's second division and Custer's brigade of the third division of Union cavalry, and then and there was fought the cavalry battle of the campaign, and one of the sharpest cavalry battles of the war; it is known in history as "The Sabre Fight." Stuart was at a disadvantage; his men were worn and weary from long and continuous riding; his horses were jaded and spiritless, while Gregg's and Custer's men and horses were comparatively fresh and vigourous, and ready for action. Stuart was overcome in every charge. His lines were broken, his troopers scattered. He was defeated, and returned in haste to the rear of Lee's infantry — not Meade's, as ordered. And so it came to pass that Stuart did not charge in conjunction with Pickett and Pettigrew, when the thunder of Lee's artillery ceased.

CHAPTER XXII

THE GREAT CANNONADE

THE second act in Lee's programme for July third began at about a quarter past one o'clock in the afternoon. Lee's orders had been obeyed to the letter, and every battery and every gun on Seminary Ridge of sufficient range to reach Meade's position had been carefully posted and trained upon his left centre.

The whole supervision of the battle had been put into the hands of Longstreet; to which he seems to have objected, for he says: "General Lee knew that I did not believe that success was possible, and he should have put an officer in charge who had more confidence in his plan. Two-thirds of the troops were of other commands, and there was no reason for putting the assaulting forces under my charge. He had confidence in General Early, who had advised in favour of that point of the line of battle. Knowing my want of confidence, he should have given the benefit of his presence and his assistance in getting the troops up, posting them, and arranging the batteries; but he gave no orders or suggestions after his early designation of the point for which the column should march."

This was surely placing Longstreet in a trying position; and feeling in his soul that it would be a useless sacrifice, he arranged the details with a heavy heart. As the assault and the cannonade were both under the general direction of Longstreet, there can be given no more correct information of the preparations made, than by quoting his own words; and here is what he says:

"The director of the artillery was asked to select a position in his line from which he could note the effect of his practice, and to advise General Pickett when the enemy's fire was so disturbed as to call for the assault. General Pickett's was the division of direction, and he was ordered to have a staff officer or courier with the artillery director to bear notice of the movement to advance."

To show what an eminent Confederate officer of artillery thought of the chances for success, and what was the true condition of their ammunition supply when the artillery duel began, we make these further quotations from Longstreet's account:

"When satisfied that the work of preparation was all that it could be from the means at hand, I wrote Colonel Walton, of the Washington Artillery:

'Colonel: 'Head-quarters, July third, 1863.

'Let the batteries open.   Order great care and precision in firing.   When the batteries at the Peach Orchard cannot be used against the point we intend to attack, let them open on the enemy on the rocky hill.

'Most respectfully,
'James Longstreet,
'Lieutenant-General Commanding.'

"At the same time a note to Alexander directed that Pickett should not be called until the artillery practice indicated fair opportunity.   In a few minutes report came from Alexander that he would only be able to judge of the effect of the fire by the return of that of the enemy, as his infantry was not exposed to view, and the smoke of the batteries would soon cover the field.

"Alexander asked if there was an alternative that it be carefully considered before the batteries opened, as there *was not* enough artillery ammunition for this and another trial, if this should not prove favourable.

"He was informed that there was no alternative; that I could find no way out of it; that General Lee had considered and would listen to nothing else; that orders had gone for the guns to give signal for the batteries to open; that he should call the troops at the first opportunity or lull in the enemy's fire."

Then the signal gun sounded, and the silence which for two hours or more had brooded over the field was broken by the Washington Artillery of New Orleans, which was posted in the edge of the woods on Seminary Ridge, nearly opposite the Union left-centre, and then the whole ridge up and down for the distance of a mile and a half lighted up with one continuous blaze, as gun after gun and battery after battery opened their ponderous throats, belching forth fire and messengers of death and destruction.

It was a grand and awful demonstration of military buncombe; useless, foolish, and costly on the part of and for the general that planned and ordered it; but it demonstrated one fact beyond all question, which is, that Lee was not so weak in men and material, and the Confederacy was not so destitute of the sinews of war, as their historians and friends, both South and North, would have the world believe.

Lee was a long way from home, and from his base of supplies, yet he developed a strength of artillery in that cannonade that surprised Meade.

GETTYSBURG

If Lee was putting up a bluff for Meade's benefit and consideration, it should have ended there, and he should have retreated without any further sacrifice of life. But it cannot be claimed honestly for an army that it is inferior in numbers and war-material to its adversary, when it is able to concentrate on a given point from one hundred to one hundred and twenty pieces of long-range heavy field-artillery, while that adversary is able to reply with but eighty or ninety guns; and that was the situation on the third of July. But it would have been wiser for Lee to save his ammunition. Of course there was immense damage done on both sides during that great military duel, the greatest probably that ever took place on the American continent; it lasted for an hour and a half, or more, or until well along toward three o'clock. Caissons were blown up, guns dismounted and disabled, batteries silenced, trees splintered, rocks riven, horses and men killed and wounded, but it had no effect whatever on the general result of the charge in contemplation. If Lee expected to retreat, as he afterwards did, and was burdened with an overweight of ammunition that he was anxious to dispose of (which is not at all likely), then this grand cannonade was a display of wisdom on his part; for the only possible advantage he could have gained by this squandering of his ammunition by the ton, was, that his limber-chests, caissons, and ammunition wagons were lightened for retreat.

On the other hand, if Lee expected to have any use for ammunition on the retreat, or ever after, or if it was a fact that the Confederate Government was sore pressed to procure the very stores that he so lavishly threw away and wasted, then it was another of the great blunders of a great general.

While Lee had the advantage in the number of guns engaged (which in the matter of expending ammunition proved to be only a disadvantage), and also in the positions of his batteries, Seminary Ridge being heavily wooded and thus furnishing ample cover for his caissons and horses in rear of his guns, Meade had the advantage in reserves with which to replace his crippled and exhausted batteries, and a decided advantage in the fact that his Chief-of-Artillery, General Hunt, foresaw that the cannonade was but the prelude to some act that was being arranged behind the scenes, and in good time to make ample preparation to meet it. Usually a cannonade directed against an infantry line can be for but one purpose only — to disturb and rattle the infantry so that their lines may be the easier penetrated by a charging column; but in this instance Longstreet's main object was, undoubtedly, to silence and disable as far as possible the Union artillery on Cemetery Hill and the ridge back of Hancock's centre, that commanded the ground over which the contemplated Confederate charge was to be made; for during its continuance he says:

"General Pickett rode to confer with Alexander, then on the ground upon which I was resting, where he was soon handed a slip of paper. After reading it he handed it to me. It read:

"'If you are coming at all, come at once, or I cannot give you proper support; but the enemy's fire has not slackened at all. At least eighteen guns are still firing from the Cemetery itself. ALEXANDER.'

"I mounted and spurred for Alexander's post. He reported that the ammunition of the batteries of position was so reduced that he could not use them in proper support of the infantry. He was ordered to fill up his ammunition-chests. But alas! there was no more ammunition to be had.

GETTYSBURG

"Just then a number of the enemy's batteries hitched up and hauled off, which gave a glimpse of unexpected hope."

This was at the time that Hunt ordered the long-range Union guns to cease firing. The concentration of the Confederate fire on this point plainly told where the charge was intended to strike, and in order to be ready to meet it, Hunt ordered the Union guns to cease firing. This was what gave Longstreet and his Confederates "a glimpse of unexpected hope," hope that their stupendous artillery effort had had some effect on the Union batteries. But that Longstreet was deceived by this timely precaution on the part of Hunt, there is grave doubt. He might have hoped that the grandest artillery demonstration ever ordered by his great Commander, Lee, had accomplished more than it did, but he was too good a soldier to suppose for a' moment that Meade was out of ammunition, or all the batteries along his lines disabled. The movement afforded him only "a glimpse of hope."

How meagre that glimpse really was, the sequel proved. Hunt was only changing guns. While the preparations for the great Confederate charge that was to break the Union centre and defeat and destroy the Army of the Potomac went on, and as the Confederate batteries, hot from excessive action and almost exhausted of ammunition, ceased firing, Hunt filled the places of his retired batteries on every hill and commanding eminence with short-range guns — brass twelve-pounders, howitzers, and Napoleons, to repel infantry — with enough rifle batteries — Parrotts and Rodmans — to reach out to meet them early in their advance, and to hold their batteries level; and the beauty of it all was that Hunt's guns were cool and in perfect order, and his artillerymen fresh and eager for the fray.

Steinwehr, on the west front of Cemetery Hill, was ready; Doubleday on its southern trend, was ready; Hancock, far down the ridge, was ready; Hunt, on every knoll where a battery of artillery could be placed, was ready.

The great cannonade was at an end. The infantry had not been shaken. The artillery had not been disabled. The whole Union line was intact, awaiting with confidence the last act of the drama of battle.

CHAPTER XXIII

PICKETT'S CHARGE

IN order to give the reader a correct idea as well as a truthful account of the Confederate formation for that charge, which history has falsely assumed was the main feature of the Battle of Gettysburg and the danger-hour in the life of the nation, we will accept Longstreet's report, for he, above all others, is the man who should know. In his report of the charge, he says: "As the commands reported, Pickett was assigned on the right, Kemper's and Garnett's brigades to be supported by Armistead's. Wilcox's brigade of the Third Corps in *échelon* and guarding Pickett's right; Pettigrew's division on Pickett's left, supported by the brigades of Scales and Lane, and under command of General Trimble. The brigades of Pettigrew's division were Archer's, Pettigrew's, Brockenbrough's, and Davis's."

Thus the attacking force comprised two columns, two lines in depth; Pickett on the right, his flank guarded by one brigade. Pickett's fifteen regiments were all Virginians, Wilcox's five regiments were all Alabamans,— twenty regiments in all in the column. Pettigrew's column on the left comprised four brigades, somewhat mixed in statality, as it comprised five North Carolinian regiments, four Virginian, three Tennesseean, three Mississippian, and one Alabaman, or sixteen in all. Pettigrew's two supporting brigades comprising ten regiments, all of which were North Carolinians; so that, of Pettigrew's column, fifteen of his twenty-six regiments hailed from the old North State. In the right column, then, the majority were from Virginia; in the left column a majority represented North Carolina. This fact occasioned no dispute or trouble between them on the third of July, 1863, but in after years it was the source of much bickering among the survivors of the lost cause.

Longstreet does not give the strength of either of these columns, but says, of his conversation with Lee earlier in the day, when he indicated the point to which the charge should be directed: "I asked the strength of the column. Lee stated 15,000. I expressed the opinion that the 15,000 men who could make successful assault over that field had never been arrayed in battle; but he was impatient of listening and tired of talking, and nothing was left but to proceed."

It might be presumed that the column was strengthened on such a pointed expression of lack of confidence in its sufficiency by the man who was to direct it to victory or defeat, before the final arrangements were made. Later in his account Longstreet says: "Two-thirds of the troops were of other commands." As Pickett's division was of his command and comprised six thousand men, it is quite reasonable to believe that there were about eighteen thousand in the two columns. And there we will leave it, anywhere between Lee's and Longstreet's estimates.

General Pickett's division numbered 6,114 present, equipped for duty, on June twentieth, the last return of which we have record made by Pickett previous to the Battle of Gettysburg, and it could not have fallen below six thousand when it started out in lead of the column of direction on that immortal charge in the afternoon of July third.

These columns were in readiness to move forward, and as the propitious moment arrived when Hunt drew off his heated batteries, giving the Confederates a "glimpse of unexpected hope," Longstreet describes the last moment of waiting and the final order for action as follows: "Pickett said, 'General, shall I advance?' The effort to speak the order failed, and I could only indicate it by an affirmative bow. He accepted the duty with seeming confidence of success, leaped on his horse and rode gayly to his command."

This force — these two columns, whatever their numbers may have been — was the force that Lee had selected to strike the Army of the Potomac in the centre and split it wide open. Was there ever an act more foolhardy, more unworthy the genius of a great general? Longstreet gives it as his opinion that, "Forty thousand men, unsupported as we were, could not have carried that position at Gettysburg. The enemy was there. Officers and men knew their advantage, and were resolved to stay until the hills came down over them. It is simply out of the question for a lesser force to march over broad, open fields and carry a fortified front occupied by a greater force of seasoned troops."

In another place, speaking of his better chances of success by weakening his right to increase the strength of Pickett's column, he says: "Had the column been augmented by the divisions of my right, its brave men might have penetrated far enough to reach Johnson's Island as prisoners; their return to General Lee by any other route is unlikely."

Lee ordered that Pickett should be strongly supported, but it is possible that the supports furnished were not equal to the division of direction in spirit, for in his whole army it was impossible to find supports who had not been there before, many of them more than once on that same fatal battlefield, or near by, and it was not strange that their enthusiasm was not at the white heat that seemed to glow and burn in the hearts of Pickett's men.

GETTYSBURG

From the edge of the woods on Seminary Ridge, where the Confederates came out from their shelter, to the umbrella-shaped copse on Cemetery Ridge beyond the valley selected for Pickett's objective, is little short of a mile and a quarter. The course of the march crosses the valley and the Emmetsburg Road north of the Codori House, and the two columns, each occupying a frontage of two brigades and supported on either flank by a still farther extension of frontage, covered a space of three-fourths of a mile from north to south. Along this frontage Seminary Ridge slopes rapidly to the eastward for the first three hundred yards, then for a thousand yards the valley is undulating with a perceptible rise along the Emmetsburg Road about two-thirds or three-fourths of the distance across, the trend of the road being toward Cemetery Hill as one goes northward, then a gentle slope upward for the last two or three hundred yards which increases in sharpness to the north, rising abruptly to Cemetery Hill.

The hill itself, which overlooks all this valley, presented one continuous front of artillery, and the ridge southward and every knoll of commanding eminence behind it was studded with cannon; while in front and below the frowning batteries, gleaming lines of steel along the tawny earthworks told where patiently the infantry bided their time.

When Longstreet, who foresaw the slaughter and opposed the charge, looked out over that wide valley and beheld the far side thereof, with its frowning ridges and glimmering labyrinths, where death and destruction watched and waited, what wonder that his voice failed him, and, as one struck dumb with sorrow for the useless sacrifice of his brave soldiers, answered only with a nod of assent when Pickett saluted him and asked, " Shall I lead my command forward ? "

Within from ten to fifteen minutes after the artillery ceased firing, Pickett's brave Virginians and Pettigrew's heroic North Carolinians, with their brother clans equally brave and heroic, marched out of the woods with their guns at a right-shoulder, and with steady, measured tread, as if on parade, headed down the eastern slope of Seminary Ridge and straight for the " jaws of death " ! When the rear line of the double column was well out of the woods, presenting a splendid mark thus silhouetted against the face of the ridge, Cemetery Hill and all the ridge southward blazed and thundered anew, concentrating an appalling fire on the advancing forces. Such is war! Still on the Confederates came. When they reached the Emmetsburg Road they entered the "mouth of hell," for then the twelve-pounders and light field-guns loaded with canister which the gunners double-shotted as the columns advanced, came into action, and the musketry from outlying rifle-pits were in reach. Here the fury and destructiveness of the battle reached its height. The charging Confederates here began first to use their muskets, and return the Union fire.

As the old veteran was not where he could see this charge, though within hearing distance of the battle, we will quote from "The Cannoneer," who was a gunner of Battery B, Fourth United States Artillery, and saw the charge with his own eyes:

"At this instant the scene down to the left, where the main line was charging, reached its climax. Every gun in our lines that could reach them was going, and owing to the openness of the level ground they had to cross, frightful execution was done at every step. As we could not fire after they got within range of our guns, without firing along the front of our own line, and as the force in our front was not yet within easy range, we had nothing to do but look on. Meantime the advance line of the charging forces had got across the level ground and had begun to climb the slope of Cemetery Ridge. This brought them into contact with our advanced skirmishers, who lined every stone wall, clump of bushes, and boulder in the fields along the Emmetsburg Road, and who opened a deadly fusillade.

" Then, for the first time the charging troops began to use their muskets. It was now about four o'clock, and though the sinking sun was shining bright and hot, the enormous amount of smoke that had drifted over to the westward made the air seem like one of those soft, hazy days as seen in Indian Summer; but the peacefulness of nature found no response. On the contrary, the whole expanse between the two ridges was a pandemonium of yelling soldiers, flashing muskets, shells bursting in air and on the ground, riderless horses tearing about, barns, houses, and haystacks on fire — everywhere flame, smoke, and every other evidence of destruction; while above all was the stupendous uproar of a hundred cannon, 30,000 muskets, and myriads of bursting shells — the whole making one ceaseless crash, as if the world was breaking up! "

It is from this point of the battle onward that the North Carolinians of Pettigrew's column claim to have been defrauded by the Virginians of their full share of the glory won that day. We are inclined to the belief that the glory of their defeat is hardly worth quarrelling about; and as it is a matter concerning their own funeral upon which they have a right to disagree, we are interested only so far as the truth of history is involved.

However, it does seem to us that history, poetry, and romance have combined to give Pickett's column credit for the whole affair. The truth is that both columns reached the Emmetsburg Road and opened fire on the intrenched Union troops; and from that moment the battle was desperate until the Confederates gave way, which did not exceed twenty minutes. Pettigrew's column, being to the north or left, came squarely up against the west front of Cemetery Hill, which is steep and rugged; while Pickett's column was directed against a gently sloping ridge much easier of ascent, and no better defended by both artillery and infantry.

The fact that the west front of Cemetery Hill was defended by Steinwehr's division of the Eleventh Corps, comprising two brigades, Coster's and Smith's, the latter not having engaged in battle on the first or second of July, and that Smith's brigade lost then and there 348 men, is proof positive that Pettigrew's column did some effective shooting. Coster's brigade lost 597, eight-tenths of which were lost in this battle of the third; and when a division of three thousand men loses over eight hundred in less than half an hour's fighting, it must be admitted that they were up against soldiers who did not care whom they hit. More than that, on the left of Steinwehr, between him and Hancock, where the front was less abrupt, were stationed the second and third divisions of the First Corps, the two being about equal in strength to Steinwehr's; therefore Cemetery Hill was defended by about six thousand Union infantry, and Pettigrew's North Carolinians and their fellows from the South made it mighty hot for them for that short half-hour. Pettigrew and Trimble were both wounded, the latter severely. Longstreet speaks in high praise of Pettigrew and Trimble, and the officers and men of their column.

Longstreet tells us that here at the Emmetsburg Road, or while both columns were advancing or trying to advance under this frightful fire, " General Pickett, finding the battle broken, called the troops off." It does not appear that Pickett had much to do with calling off the troops of either column, but it does appear that he led his column no farther than the Emmetsburg Road, and that the great majority of the soldiers of both columns, finding it impossible to stem the fierce tide of battle beyond that line, with one accord followed Pickett back to the shelter of Seminary Ridge, and were quite lively about it.

Armistead of the second line pressed forward, gathering up his shattered remnants for a final effort; and herein Pickett's column carried off the palm of glory. In face of that awful death-storm, they reached the foot of the ridge. Now they are climbing the slope: Lee shall not think — the world shall never say — that the fault of defeat was theirs. Two hundred yards farther is the copse on the crest of the ridge, a hundred yards only to Hancock's waiting lines of infantry. Then the crash of musketry increases to a sound like falling forests, and the charging lines melt away as snow before the breath of the Chinook. Kemper is wounded; Garnett is killed; Armistead puts his cap on the point of his sword to guide his devoted band; he leaps the outer wall and falls within the Union line. The force of the charge is spent; they cannot retreat; they are at the end of their march; they throw down their arms and surrender, all that is left of them. Pickett's mad charge, the last act in the great tragedy among the picturesque hills of Gettysburg, is over.

During the advance of the Confederate columns across the valley, their artillery was not by any means idle, and wherever they had ammunition they used it freely, giving the Union artillery and infantry, also, the very best (or worst) that was at their command. Although the advantages were all with the Army of the Potomac, even then the battle was not all on one side.

General Hancock, General Gibbon, and General Stannard were wounded during the engagement, and Lieutenant Cushing — commanding Battery A, Fourth U. S. Artillery — was killed, while working the last serviceable gun of his battery, about fifty yards to the right and front of the umbrella-shaped copse, within a few feet of the spot where the Confederate Armistead fell riddled with bullets.

This point, called the "Bloody Angle," was so named from the fact that here culminated Pickett's Charge, at a point about seventy-five yards in advance of the general line on either side, being defended in front and on the right and left by a stone wall, on each of three sides, over the front wall of which Armistead and a few of his followers leaped to their deaths. This was the only point where any of Pickett's men got within the Union lines; and not one of them ever got out again except as a war-prisoner.

Pickett's division was said to have been annihilated, but though his losses were heavy the percentage was not equal to that of some Union brigades in the previous days of the battle. Of four generals and fifteen field officers, only Pickett and one lieutenant-colonel returned to Seminary Ridge unharmed.

When it was known that the Confederate charge had failed, General Kilpatrick sent his first brigade, commanded by General Farnsworth, on a charge through the infantry detachments in rear of the Confederate right. Presumably the order came from General Meade. Farnsworth made a heroic charge, riding over rocks and stone fences, cutting his way through detachments of guards, and riding down the skirmishers that opposed him, but was obliged at several points to come under infantry and artillery fire, where he was finally killed, and his brigade defeated and turned back with heavy loss.

The demonstration was uncalled for and foolish in the extreme, for the reason that it was a useless waste of life, as Meade had no infantry in readiness to support the cavalry. Longstreet says of that charge: "Had the ride been followed promptly by the enemy's infantry, and pushed with vigour, they could have reached our line of retreat."

By four o'clock P.M. the great Battle of Gettysburg was over. Lee and Meade faced each other in battle-line until the morning of July fifth, but during all that time Lee was hustling his trains, his wounded, and his war-prisoners, over the Hagerstown and Chambersburg Roads toward the Potomac.

CHAPTER XXIV

GETTYSBURG TO APPOMATTOX

WHEN the Battle of Gettysburg was over, Meade's lines were all intact, and he had a concentrated army of about 70,000 men, of all arms, under his command. The losses sustained by the Army of the Potomac during the three days at Gettysburg, and including the cavalry losses in their battles immediately around Gettysburg, are officially stated as follows:

General Headquarters . . .	4
First Corps	6,024
Second Corps	4,350
Third Corps	4,210
Fifth Corps	2,187
Sixth Corps	242
Eleventh Corps	3,801
Twelfth Corps	1,081
Artillery Reserve	242
Cavalry Corps	849
Total loss of all arms . . .	22,990

These figures leave the strength of the various corps and of the army when the battle was over, as follows:

First Corps	3,998
Second Corps	8,558
Third Corps	7,714
Fifth Corps	10,322
Sixth Corps	15,313
Eleventh Corps	6,040
Twelfth Corps	7,508
Reserve Artillery	2,304
Cavalry Corps	9,951
Total of all arms	71,708

As these figures make no allowance for loss by sickness during the days of the battle, it seems fair to assume that Meade's army, after the Battle of Gettysburg was ended, stood on that ridge of hills confronting Lee, 70,000 strong. It is not by any means so easy to fix the strength of Lee's army, as his losses never were and never can be ascertained with any degree of accuracy. The Confederate losses, as given by Longstreet, which agree pretty closely with all Confederate guess-work reports, are as accurate as any to be obtained, and are as follows:

GETTYSBURG

Longstreet's First Corps . . . 7,539
Ewell's Second Corps . . . 5,937
Hill's Third Corps 6,735
Cavalry Corps 1,426

Total loss of all arms . . . 21,637

This difference of 1,353 in favour of the Confederates, if true, shows that Lee really retreated from Gettysburg with undue haste, for his army must have been, as compared with Meade's, better able to remain in Pennsylvania and continue his campaign against Washington than when he invaded the North. Lee may have been short of ammunition on account of his lavish waste of it at the great cannonade, and may have been compelled to retreat on that account, but from the Confederate showing there can be no other reason. However, we are inclined to believe that the Confederate losses in the aggregate exceeded the Union losses by several thousand. In the matter of prisoners alone there is a discrepancy sufficiently wide to make a very different showing. While the Confederates report a loss of 5,150 as missing and unaccounted for, it is a fact that the record of war-prisoners on file in the office of the Adjutant General of the United States Army bears the names of 12,227 wounded and unwounded Confederates captured at Gettysburg between July first and fifth inclusive. There we find a difference of 7,077. It is not possible that a third more than half of the prisoners taken by the Union forces were wounded men. Neither is it possible that the Confederates had any means of knowing what proportion of their missing were wounded. They claim to have lost in wounded 12,700, so that if all the prisoners captured by the Union forces were in excess of 5,150 — which the Confederates claim as the extent of their missing — then it must appear that of their 12,700 wounded the Union forces captured 7,077, while they retained and carried with them back to Virginia but 5,623 of their wounded. Such an outcome must have been impossible at Gettysburg, for in no instance did the Union army capture a Confederate hospital and it was only the desperately wounded that the Confederates could not remove that fell into our hands. In every battle three-fourths of the wounded can care for themselves, and more than half are only slightly wounded. From the battlefields of Gettysburg the Confederates took with them at least three-fourths of their wounded. If we count the prisoners actually taken by the Union forces, it adds to their losses 7,077 in missing, swelling the Confederate aggregate loss to 28,714.

If the Confederate reports are true, our loss in killed and wounded exceeded theirs by 2,482.

The percentages of Union losses in the various battles can be closely estimated, and were about as follows: In the battle of July first, the longest, most stubbornly contested of the series of battles, and the only one wherein the Confederates were victorious, the Union loss was 41 per cent. In the main battle of July second, which includes Peach Orchard, the Wheatfield, and Little Round Top, the Union loss was 30 per cent. In Early's charge on Cemetery Hill on the evening of July second, the Union loss was 16 per cent. In Slocum's battle on the right, including both Greene's engagement on the evening of July second and the main battle on the morning of July third, wherein Slocum regained his lost position, Slocum's loss was 12 per cent.

In Pickett's Charge, on July third, a careful estimate places the number of Union troops defending the left centre of Meade's lines approximately at eleven thousand, with an approximate loss of 24 per cent.

It is impossible to ascertain the Confederate percentage of losses; but if Longstreet's statement is correct relative to his battle on the left on July second, — that he made the battle with 17,000 men and that his loss was 6,000, — it would amount in that instance to about 35 per cent. On the other hand, if our estimate is the correct one, and Longstreet had 26,000 and lost about 9,000 in the battle, then the percentage of his loss was about the same, or 34 per cent.

In Pickett's Charge the Confederate account places Pickett's loss as follows:

Kemper's brigade	.	.	.	731
Garnett's brigade	.	.	.	941
Armistead's brigade.		.	.	1,191
Pickett's *total loss*	.	.	.	2,863

or forty per cent.

It is useless, in fact wearisome, to pursue this estimate of losses farther. Each army lost more than it could afford to lose; and we speak of the losses in this connection on account of their bearing on the campaigns that followed.

The Confederates, living and dead, and their descendants, have no reason to be ashamed of their prowess as soldiers at Gettysburg, and at other great battles, so far as their fighting qualities were concerned, for they were magnificent fighters, there is no question about that.

Therefore, it seems foolish for them to try to deny their great losses and Lee's terrible blunders at Gettysburg, in order to save the reputation of Lee as a military genius. At Fredericksburg, Burnside assaulted Lee's position, which was not less secure and impregnable than Meade's was at Gettysburg, the principal difference being that Lee had his army all concentrated and in position at Fredericksburg before the battle opened. There Burnside's loss was 12,321, to Lee's 5,309, as reported by him, or more than two to one; but the

United States did not belie its losses, either on that account, or to save Burnside's reputation. Lee made military blunders at Gettysburg that were not exceeded by Burnside at Fredericksburg; and it seems perfectly foolish for Lee's admirers, South or North, to befog and belie the truths of history.

After the battle, and during the remainder of the third and all of the fourth of July, with an army of 70,000 men under his command, 15,000 of whom, or one-fourth of his infantry (the Sixth Corps), having scarcely pulled a trigger during the battle, Meade watched Lee pull his defeated army together, which had been pounded, and hammered, and slaughtered, and repulsed at every point, and march away with flying colors to prolong the war for another year and a half. It should have ended immediately after the Confederate authorities learned of the utter failure of that campaign.

Gettysburg was Meade's first and last battle as a commanding general. He retained the supreme command of the Army of the Potomac until the next winter, and handled it skilfully in avoiding battle, but made no headway toward overthrowing the Confederacy. He retained command of the Army of the Potomac under Grant until after Appomattox and the close of the war, and proved himself to be a skilful and reliable lieutenant in executing the plans of a competent leader; but if the United States had given him an army of 500,000 men, and allowed him to retain the chief command of that army, it is very doubtful if he ever would have taken Richmond, or captured Lee's army. Meade was far from being a great general. Appomattox was the complement of Gettysburg. Without a Gettysburg, Appomattox never could have been reached; and without an Appomattox, Gettysburg and all the other battles of the Civil War would have been in vain.

Gettysburg was the death-warrant of the Southern Confederacy and of slavery. Appomattox was the execution of the former and the death-knell of the latter.

When the Southern Confederacy died, Abraham Lincoln's Emancipation Proclamation had the power to free, and did free, every slave beneath the

GETTYSBURG

Stars and Stripes; and the God-accursed institution that had dominated America for more than two hundred years, and finally drenched the land with blood, met the death that it deserved.

CHAPTER XXV

ABOUT three hundred and fifty yards south of the steel tower on South Cemetery Hill, stands the little umbrella thicket or grove that guided Pickett in his last mad charge on Hancock's lines on the afternoon of July third, 1863.

The grove stands on the west side of Hancock Avenue, and consists of forty trees — thirty rock-oaks, nine red-oaks, and one hickory. They stand on a rocky knob in a thick cluster, which causes their branches to spread out like a great umbrella.

The grove is enclosed by an iron picket fence, in a circle sixty yards in circumference. Seven hundred and fifty yards south of this grove, on the west side of Hancock Avenue, stands the monument of the First Minnesota Infantry, the first among the infantry of the armies of the United States in the Civil War. Of all the regiments that participated in the Battle of Gettysburg on either side, the First Minnesota deserves the highest honour for bravery, firmness, endurance, and success.

Not on another field of war since the world began was ever exhibited a more daring and heroic deed than that performed by the First Minnesota in front of that monument, on the afternoon of July second.

At a critical moment when the tempest of battle was raging in its fury over and around the Wheatfield; when the Confederates had broken through Caldwell's lines, and Wright's brigade was advancing toward the crest of Cemetery Ridge; in order to gain the necessary time to interpose a brigade from Sykes' oncoming corps, General Hancock ordered a single regiment — the First Minnesota, which was the only one obtainable — to charge in and delay the advancing foe. The regiment advanced with two hundred and sixty-two men in line, meeting a brigade of the enemy and losing within the space of fifteen minutes two hundred and twenty-five in killed and wounded, or eighty-six per cent of their whole number; but they checked the Confederate advance and held their ground against them until Hancock was enabled to supply reinforcements.

Here was a display of heroism and endurance that threw Pickett's Charge of the following day far into the shade. The charge of the Six Hundred at Balaklava, October twenty-fifth, 1854, and the charge of Pickett's six thousand at Gettysburg on the third of July, 1863, were both surpassed by the charge of this less than three hundred at Gettysburg on the second of July, 1863; for there the brave Minnesotans accomplished what they undertook. Both Lord Cardigan's charge with his Light Brigade, and Pickett's Charge with his three brigades were failures, the latter being a terrible defeat; but the charge of the First Minnesota was a success — a victory. They held their ground, and when the battle was over they were all there, not a man missing, every man accounted for: fifty killed, one hundred and seventy-five wounded, thirty-seven still in battle-line, and the line in their keeping.

In behalf of the Iron Brigade, which lost sixty-four per cent of its number at Gettysburg — more than any other brigade in either army; in behalf of the Second Wisconsin Infantry, which lost a larger percentage of killed and wounded than any other regiment in the Union army during the war, the old veteran respectfully takes off his hat to the First Minnesota.

CHAPTER XXVI

A T the time of the Battle of Gettysburg the Umbrella Grove, of rock-oaks mostly, was a copse, and after many years the old veteran returning to the fields of Gettysburg found it still a clump of dwarfed trees, apparently stunted in growth from the fact that it stands on a rocky knob. Just north of this grove there is what appears to have been a small field or pasture, enclosed on three sides with a stone wall, and extending to the front or westward about a hundred yards. On the day of the battle, the western wall was used for a breastwork of defence; it sheltered Hancock's infantry against Armistead's oncoming troopers. Within the enclosure (the rear wall having been removed to give place to Hancock Avenue) and thirty yards in rear of the front wall, stood Cushing's battery. A marker designates the spot where Lieutenant Cushing fell dead, as he fired his last shot. The front wall is the same over which Armistead led his followers to their doom.

This wall-enclosed square or field is called the "Bloody Angle," and is designated on the "Map and Monumental Guide of the Gettysburg Battle-fields," and by all or nearly all who have attempted to describe it, as the "high tide of Gettysburg." The visitor who journeys far to see this historic battlefield, usually procures a carriage, the driver acting as guide, and is driven out on Washington Street till it merges into the Taneytown Road, thence along that road and Hancock Avenue until this point is reached. There the guide, as he pur-ports to be, recounts his story of Pickett's awful charge and near success, with victory almost within his grasp, the Army of the Potomac on the verge of defeat and dissolution, while the life of the nation trembled in the balance, etc.; and the visitor, look-ing across the valley to the wooded crest of Semi-nary Ridge, from which Pickett's division marched forth to its doom, thinks he has seen the battle-field of Gettysburg, or at least all of it worth the seeing, and that he is actually standing on the line

—the identical spot and point—demarcating the culmination of the "high tide" of the Rebellion. But the visitor is misled; the guide is in error. Standing at the Bloody Angle the battlefields of Gettysburg are all around you, to the west, to the northwest, to the north, to the northeast, to the east, to the south, and to the southwest; in fact history is at fault, and all the poetry and eloquence expended for the past forty-seven years on Pickett's Charge as the one supreme event in American history, by which the Army of the Potomac was in imminent danger of being wiped from the face of the earth, and the life of the Republic hung by a thread, have been wasted—indeed, worse than wasted, for they have served to bury the truth of history beneath a high tide of delusive nonsense.

All about the umbrella copse and within the wall-enclosed field where Cushing's battery stood, and outside the wall far down the valley to the Emmetsburg Road and beyond, was bloody enough on that third day of July, 1863, but there were dozens of other angles on the fields and hillsides and in the valleys around Gettysburg, that were equally bloody; and when Pickett's mad charge was made, the danger-hour for the Army of the Potomac and for the nation that that army defended had passed fully eighteen hours before. A great writer once said, "All history is a lie," and in a measure that statement is true. No better proof of that truth can be cited than the fact that poets, historians, orators, map-makers, monument-makers, guides, and visitors of this great battlefield, have all fallen readily into the same rut of untruth, outlined by the first despatch from Gettysburg after the hard-won victory was fully assured, that the danger-point was the umbrella copse and the danger-hour the time of Pickett's Charge, successfully repelled.

The object, therefore, of this chapter is to correct that error, if such may now be possible, while some who participated in the great battle are still living and can testify to the truth of the statements herein contained.

That the "high tide" of the Confederacy culminated at Gettysburg, there can be no dispute. Lee's army was then at the zenith of its power, and opened the battle in full confidence of its strength and ability to win a sweeping and far-reaching victory. From every reasonable human standpoint, Lee should have won the Battle of Gettysburg. He commanded a powerful and previously victorious army, and the confidence and faith of every officer and every soldier of that army in the wise generalship and supreme genius of their leader amounted to a superstition.

In the battle of July first Lee's "high tide" of victory culminated, sweeping the Union army from the field, and it looked very much as though he were destined to accomplish all that the Richmond oligarchy expected from him. In the battle of the second of July there was no "high tide" of victory for either army; but there was an appalling danger from the Confederate battle-line, rolling in against the Union front, like a mighty surge of the sea, from Little Round Top to Rock Creek.

The danger-hour and the bloody sunset hour of that terrible day were one and the same. There we find the "high tide" of the Confederacy, not only for Gettysburg but for the war, when the vortex of battle surged up toward Cemetery Ridge; when

Sickles and Brooke, bleeding and disabled, were out of the fight, and Willard, Sherill, Cross, and Zook lay dead on the trampled and gory Wheatfield; when Weed, Vincent, O'Rorke, and Hazlett were dying to save Little Round Top; when the First Minnesota Infantry stood in the death-laden breach and blocked the Confederate advance with their dead and dying comrades; when the belching guns of the Fourth United States and Fifth Maine Batteries were sweeping Early's Tigers from the gates of the Cemetery, and Sprigg Carroll's brigade was dashing over rocks at a double, to reinforce Von Gilsa's recoiling troops; when Greene with but one brigade was holding Culp's Hill, around which the spume of that surging tide lay until the next day, against Johnson's division; while Slocum, leaving the right in peril, was hurrying away to relieve the left from apparently a greater peril. That was the "high tide" of danger for America and Freedom; the bloody sunset for Lee.

And what about Pickett's Charge, on the third day of July, the tragic third act of this most spectacular drama of battle, so frequently called the Confederate "high tide" at Gettysburg? As well call the last stand of the Old Guard at La Haye Sainte, Napoleon's high tide at Waterloo, for that was Napoleon's high tide of defeat. But there was need for the Old Guard to die! The Prussians on their flank and the English from Mont St. Jean were advancing in wild triumph and unbroken ranks, sweeping the French battalions like chaff before the wind. They went to their doom bravely, even cheerfully, shouting *"Vive l' Empereur!"* — recognizing the necessity of the sacrifice. They could not stem the victorious tide, but they died heroically, thereby saving the life of their great Emperor for a more humiliating and cruel fate. They could not save his cause. There was no such need, no necessity whatever for the sacrifice of Pickett's and Pettigrew's divisions by Lee, for his life was not in danger, nor his liberty at stake; though his cause on that field, and all future fields, was lost beyond redemption, his position on Seminary Ridge was secure, and his road open for a safe retreat. Pickett's double column went to their doom as bravely as Napoleon's Old Guard. They passed through the " jaws of death " and into the "mouth of hell."

Not more than fifty of Pickett's six thousand reached the Bloody Angle in front and just to the north of the Umbrella Grove, and followed Armistead over the stone wall, Hancock's outmost line, into the enclosure; and not one of that fifty returned to Seminary Ridge to tell Pickett or Longstreet or Lee the story of his adventure.

Longstreet knew it was butchery, not war, and wept as he saw his brave soldiers sent to their doom. In his normal condition of mind Lee would have recognized at once the fact known to every other officer and every soldier in his army, eighteen hours before, that the Battle of Gettysburg was irretrievably lost to him; but the finger of God, seemingly, had paralyzed his brain or stricken his soul with the madness of desire to snatch victory from defeat.

When Pickett's division was annihilated, and the victory assured to the Union army, then, and not till then, Lee recognized the fact that his defeat had swept him forever from the fulfilment of his dream, and he turned to the Hagerstown Road and the land beyond the Potomac.

APPENDIX

IN the days of the great battle there was but one tower of observation within the city that served the purpose of a viewpoint of the battlefields. That tower was the cupola of the Seminary on Seminary Ridge, and was used by General Buford, General Reynolds, and General Howard on the first day of July, and by Lee on the second and third, to view therefrom not only their own, but the enemy's lines.

Now there are, besides the cupola, five steel towers, ranging from sixty-five to seventy-five feet in height, standing on the most prominent points of elevation overlooking the old battlefields of Gettysburg.

These towers were erected by the Government, at a cost of fifty thousand dollars, expressly for observation purposes, and the grand and far-reaching views to be obtained from their summits should not be overlooked or neglected by any person who

may have the good fortune to visit this greatest
of American battlefields.

I

It was a lovely morning in May, many years
after the war, when all nature was clothed afresh in
the garments of renewed life and vigour, that we
wended our way from out the peaceful city, along
the Mummasburg Road to the point where it
crosses the Seminary Ridge, and there ascended the
tower, that from this central position overlooks the
battlefield of July first, 1863.

Standing on the summit of that tower we looked
southward, far down Seminary Ridge and Reynolds Avenue, to its point of termination, and then
westward over Buford Avenue and Reynolds'
Woods to Willoughby Run and the wooded hills
beyond. Eastward Howard Avenue crosses the
valley from the Mummasburg Road below, to Rock
Creek; and southeastward lies Gettysburg in beauty
and in peace.

The battle-lines held by the old First Corps on
July first, and especially where with our brigade

we fought from the eastern edge of Reynolds' Woods to and beyond Willoughby Run; then back again through Reynolds' Woods to Seminary Ridge, where we repulsed Heth's last charge, were full of glorious though sad recollections. Along those grand ridges, beside those sparkling waters, and on those green and grassy slopes, thousands of our comrades endured wounds and suffered death that other summer day, that seems almost but yesterday.

There war in all his fury reigned supreme. The smoke of battle hung above every hill. The victorious foe, with dancing flags on a ridge of steel, swept down the valley from the northward upon the fair city overcome with fear. To-day the city smiles in peace, the hills are fair to look upon, the orchards are fragrant with bloom, and the songs of innumerable birds fill all the air. Peace reigns o'er the land, and war is a memory of the past.

II

Descending from that tower and following the trend of Seminary Ridge southward; crossing the railroad, and the Chambersburg Pike; passing Lee's old headquarters and the Seminary with its old-time cupola; crossing the Hagerstown Road, far down Confederate Avenue we arrived at the point where the Wheatfield Road intersects Seminary Ridge. Here is the central point of observation in the Confederate battle-line of July second.

Ascending the tower, from its summit we look westward and behold the wooded slopes of Seminary Ridge and the rocky valley of Willoughby Run far below. To the eastward the wide, diversified valley stretches away to the feet of the Round Tops, heavy with the verdure of Spring, and sweet with the perfume of flowers. Before our eyes are the Emmetsburg Road, and the white monuments demarcating Humphreys' battle-line; and beyond, Cemetery Ridge, which Longstreet struggled long and desperately to reach. All is now loveliness and peace. The marks of battle have been effaced. The old Wheatfield, reaped of its appalling death-harvest, now waves with a renewed and luxuriant growth that shall not be trodden under the feet of men in the mad strife of battle; nor shall the fruit of the young Peach Orchard, now a huge bouquet of fragrant loveliness, standing where the old Peach Orchard stood in Sickles' Salient, be gathered in blood.

III

Leaving Confederate Avenue and Seminary Ridge, we follow the Wheatfield Road eastward to the Peach Orchard and Sickles' Salient; thence along the Emmetsburg Road up the valley toward the city until we reach Cemetery Hill; thence across the cemetery and along Slocum Avenue to the rocky citadel of the right. Ascending the tower that crowns Culp's Hill, and standing on the summit thereof, we see the fair city apparently beneath us to the northwest.

Northward are woodland, field, orchard, garden, and meadow. Eastward is the broken gorge, the wild valley of Rock Creek. Southward are innumerable picturesque hills, glens, rivulets, and glades. Westward we look down upon Cemetery Hill, with its imposing statues and towering monuments, and the starry flag of America waving above them. Grand and inspiring is the scene. Beneath our very feet Greene's brigade held this sublime fastness on the night of July second, against Johnson's whole division; but to-day, only the memories of war remain.

IV

Following Slocum Avenue westward, crossing the Baltimore Pike and the Cemetery to the Taneytown Road, thence southward along that road and Hancock Avenue, we reach the crest of South Cemetery Hill, overlooking the centre of the Union line of battle on July third. From the summit of this tower we can see Culp's Hill to the northeast in all his rugged glory. Northward are the cemetery and the city. Southward stretches Hancock Avenue far past the Bloody Angle and the Umbrella Grove, away to the rock-faced "key of the left" and his towering mate in the distance. South-westward the Emmetsburg Road and Sickles Avenue, with the Salient, Peach Orchard, the Wheatfield, and Death Valley, with their countless monuments, lie spread out before us like a huge map. Due west stands Seminary Ridge, extending to the north and south far as the eye can reach.

From that high ridge beyond the peaceful valley more than a mile away, across those green and flowery fields, came Pickett and Pettigrew, with their thousands of devoted followers, enveloped in the clouds of war, and marching to their death ! But the storm of battle has passed forever, and all the valley rejoices in the smiles of peace.

V

Following Hancock Avenue southward along the crest of the ridge, whose westward slopes were lapped by the ensanguined waves of the war's fierce "high tide"; crossing the massive boulders that, piled upon each other, form Little Round Top, where Vincent, Weed, O'Rorke, and Hazlett, with hundreds of their soldiers, gave their lives in full and free devotion to their country's cause, during that bloody sunset hour, we climbed the green-mantled eminence beyond and ascended the tower.

Standing seventy-five feet above the summit of the king of the rock-ribbed hills of Gettysburg, we are also lifted up in a spirit of heavenly light and joy, from which we look down upon everything that is earthly.

What a glory is Round Top! The pines and the rock-oaks clothe him in garments of green from his base to his summit, and the pilgrim above on his tower looks down o'er the sides of a mountain clothed in feathery branches. To the eastward and westward in the distance, the wooded ridges limit the vision. Southward the glorious valley stretches afar. Northward are the old battlefields — the homes of the living, the graves of the dead, the dwarfed hills, the low-lying valleys, and the far-away city.

Here all is beauty and peace! The old veteran dreams, and even the memories of war are forgotten. He forgets the past, with its strife and turmoil, forgets the present with its cares and its burdens, while within this holy temple in mid-air he communes in spirit with the Great Master!

Oh, who can describe Round Top, and paint the scene from his tower? And who can translate to mortal ears the voices, there heard by the spirit?

GETTYSBURG

A T the time of the great battle the City Cemetery stood where it still stands, its northern boundary extending across or near the summit of Cemetery Hill, while the main portion thereof occupied the southern slope. The eastern gate of the City Cemetery opened on the Baltimore Pike near the northeast corner of the enclosure, and the Baltimore Pike formed its eastern boundary, while the western boundary was formed by the Taney-town Road, on which its west gate opened. During the battle the Union line ran across Cemetery Hill, along or near the northern wall of this old City Cemetery.

North of the City Cemetery, and lying between the Baltimore Pike and Taneytown Road on a broad plateau slightly sloping toward the north, lies the National Cemetery. In the days of the battle this plateau was rough and rocky, and in a wild and uncultivated condition. The Gettysburg Cemetery

[279]

Company was organized and incorporated by the State of Pennsylvania shortly after the battle, for the purpose of establishing here a soldiers' cemetery. These grounds were dedicated for that purpose on the nineteenth of November, 1863. In 1872 the State of Pennsylvania assigned it to the Government of the United States.

The cemetery has been beautified and adorned with great care and expense, and the soldiers who died at Gettysburg in defence of the flag and the Union are buried here in sections, comprising a large semi-circular plat, each of the eighteen States represented in the battle occupying a section; beside which there in a section for United States Regulars, and a section for the Unknown Dead — which is the largest section of them all. The States represented and the number of their soldiers, the total amounting to three thousand, five hundred and fifty-three, are as follows:

Maine	104
New Hampshire	49
Vermont	61
Massachusetts	159
Rhode Island	12

GETTYSBURG

Connecticut	.	.	.	.	22
New York	.	.	.	.	861
New Jersey	.	.	.	.	78
Delaware .	.	.	.	.	15
Maryland .	.	.	.	.	22
West Virginia	.	.	.	.	11
Ohio .	.	.	.	.	131
Indiana	.	.	.	.	80
Illinois	.	.	.	.	6
Michigan .	.	.	.	.	171
Wisconsin .	.	.	.	.	73
Minnesota .	.	.	.	.	52
Pennsylvania	.	.	.	.	534
U. S. Regulars .	.	.	.	.	133
Unknown Dead	.	.	.	.	979

Among those here buried the old veteran found the name of George H. Stevens, Lieutenant-Colonel of his regiment, the Second Wisconsin; and also the names of three of his comrades of Company H — Lieutenant William S. Winegar and Privates Henry C. McCollum and Edward H. Heath; also the name of Sergeant Walter S. Rouse of Company E, all of whom were killed on July first, 1863, between Seminary Ridge and Willoughby Run. McCollum was his tentmate, and in the same file when they went into battle.

GETTYSBURG

Not all the men who died in the great battle were buried in this cemetery. Some, more especially officers, who had friends near-by that could reach the battlefield in season, were taken to their homes for burial. Some were buried where they fell, and thereafter the ground was so trodden that their graves were unrecognizable. While the old veteran was visiting the field, the skeletons of three Union soldiers were found on the hillside not far from Spangler's Spring, where the ground was being excavated for the improvement of the avenue; and probably there are many others that will never be found. Then, the old veteran was told by old men who resided in Gettysburg in the days of the battle, and after, that from Baltimore, Philadelphia, Harrisburg, Washington, and other cities, there came medical students and others seeking after subjects for the medical institutions of those cities; and beyond all doubt or question, they carried many corpses away for that purpose.

At the converging of this semicircular plat stands the Soldiers' National Monument. It is sixty feet in height and twenty-five feet square at its base, crowned with a statue representing the Genius of Liberty. Projecting from the four corners are allegorical statues representing War, History, Peace, and Plenty. Those figures were made in Italy by Randolph Rogers.

This monument was dedicated on July first, 1869, on which occasion Bayard Taylor contributed an ode; Governor Morton of Indiana delivered the oration; and General Meade made an address.

The Confederate soldiers from fourteen States, who died at Gettysburg, were buried in temporary graves, as the Union soldiers were; but later their bones were collected and carried back to the Southland, where they were finally buried; so that none but Union soldiers rest in the National Cemetery at Gettysburg.

The battlefield of Gettysburg in the hands of the United States became a National Military Park in the sense of the battle-lines being restored to and kept in the condition in which they were at the time of the battle. The work done for decorative purposes has been with the view of making the old lines more accessible. The lines of breastworks and the old buildings and stone walls, which served as land-marks at the time of the battle and were afterward destroyed, have, as far as possible, been restored to their former condition.

The Secretary of War appointed three Battle-field Commissioners, all of whom were participants in the battle. When the old veteran was on the field this Commission was composed of Colonel John P. Nicholson, Twenty-eighth Pennsylvania Infantry; Major C. A. Richardson, One Hundred and Twenty-sixth New York Infantry; Major Wm. M. Robbins, Fourth Alabama Infantry.

By Act of Congress in 1895, the battlefield became a United States Military Park, whereupon the Memorial Association transferred its grounds, amounting to about eight hundred acres, with many hundreds of beautiful monuments erected by the people of the various States, to the care and protec-tion of the United States. The battlefields in all are three miles wide by five miles long, and contain about fifteen square miles of territory. The various avenues, together with Reynolds' Woods, Culp's Hill, Spangler's Spring, Cemetery Hill, the

Umbrella Grove, Seminary Ridge, the Emmetsburg Road, the Peach Orchard, the Wheatfield, the Devil's Den, Death Valley, and the Round Tops are owned or controlled by the United States, and constitute the grandest National Park in America.

The Commission has caused to be built and opened many macadamized driveways, generally along the rear of the old battle-lines, and has marked the position of each corps, division, and brigade, so that the locations of troops on both sides may be visited in carriages.

The names of the avenues as located at the time the old veteran visited the fields were: Reynolds, Hancock, Sickles, Sykes, Sedgwick, Slocum, Howard, Meade, Buford, Pleasonton, Gregg, Kilpatrick, Devin, Merritt, Neill, Wright, Excelsior, United States, Crawford, and Brooke. Confederate Avenue, which stretches the length of Seminary Ridge, is divided and apportioned among the Confederate corps commanders, Longstreet, Ewell, Hill, and Stuart.

This park, although the best preserved and

grandest of the battlefields of the earth, is still being improved and beautified wherever possible, without disturbing any of the battle landmarks, and it is hoped that from every portion of our broad country thousands of people will visit this sacred field.

The Soldiers' National Monument, standing in a central and commanding position in the National Cemetery at Gettysburg, was formally dedicated on the first day of July, 1869.

On the very spot where stands the National Monument, stood the immortal Lincoln when he made his world-renowned Address at the dedication of the cemetery grounds on the nineteenth of November, 1863.

GETTYSBURG

LINCOLN'S GETTYSBURG ADDRESS AT THE DEDICATION
OF THE NATIONAL CEMETERY
November 19, 1863.

FOUR score and seven years ago our fathers brought forth upon this continent a new nation, conceived in liberty, and dedicated to the proposition that all men are created equal.

Now we are engaged in a great civil war, testing whether that nation or any nation so conceived and so dedicated can long endure. We are met on a great battlefield of that war. We are met to dedicate a portion of it as the final resting-place for those who here gave their lives that that nation might live. It is altogether fitting and proper that we should do this.

But, in a larger sense, we cannot dedicate, we cannot consecrate, we cannot hallow this ground. The brave men, living and dead, who struggled here have consecrated it far above our power to add or detract. The world will little note nor long remember what we say here, but it can never forget what they did here. It is for us, the living, rather, to be dedicated here to the unfinished work that they have thus far so nobly carried on. It is rather for us to be here dedicated to the great task remaining before us, that from these honoured dead we take increased devotion to that cause for which they gave the last full measure of devotion; that we here highly resolve that the dead shall not have died in vain; that this nation shall, under God, have a new birth of freedom; and that government of the people, by the people, and for the people, shall not perish from the earth.

THE END

INDEX

INDEX

[291]

INDEX

INDEX

INDEX

INDEX

Maine, Second artillery, Battery B, 80.

Maine, Third infantry, 155.

Manchester, Pa., 128.

Mansfield, Major, 88.

Marsh Creek, 45, 50.

Maryland, Second infantry, 203, 219.

Massachusetts, Fifth artillery, 166.

Massachusetts, Ninth artillery, 166, 175.

McClellan, George B. (General), 18, 19, 22.

McCollum, Henry C., 281.

McLaws' division, 153, 156, 168, 176, 177.

McPherson's Woods, *see* Reynolds' Woods.

Meade, G. C. (General), 34-36, 43-46, 50, 52, 104-106, 123, 124, 127-138, 143-149, 157, 160-163, 181-183, 194, 207, 217, 227, 229, 247, 248, 255, 256, 283.

Minnesota, First infantry, 258-261, 267.

Mississippi, regiments from, 234.

Mitchel, Sergeant, 84.

Mummasburg Road, 44, 45, 57, 75, 76.

National Monument at Gettysburg, 282, 286.

National Park at Gettysburg, 283-286.

New York, First artillery, Battery C, 165.

New York, First artillery, Battery L, 80.

New York, First infantry, 155.

New York, One Hundred and Fortieth infantry, 189.

New York, Tenth artillery, 166.

Newville Road, 57.

Nicholson, John P. (Colonel), 284.

North Carolina, regiments from, 234, 239, 241.

Northern Virginia, Army of, 16-18, 20, 21, 27-38, 53, 99, 100, 107, 108, 190, 249, 250, 253, 254, 265, 266.

Oak Hill, 76.

" Old Abe's Folly," 24.

" Old Common Sense " (General Reynolds), 122.

O'Neal's brigade, 76, 215, 220.

O'Rorke, Patrick H. (Col.), 189, 267, 277.

Packard, Corporal, 85.

Peach Orchard, 150, 164-173, 226, 252.

Pender's division, 44, 51, 71, 104, 135.

Pennsylvania, Eleventh infantry, 84.

Pennsylvania, First artillery, Battery B, 80.

Pennsylvania, First artillery, Batteries C and F, 165.

Perrins' brigade, 71.

Perry's brigade, 156.

Pettigrew's division, 70, 223, 233, 234, 239-243, 268.

INDEX

INDEX

INDEX